THE DOWAGER'S CHIHUAHUA:

Religion by the Seat of Your Pants

THE DOWAGER'S CHIHUAHUA:

Religion by the Seat of Your Pants

by
The Rt. Rev. R. Heber Gooden

UNIVERSITY OF THE SOUTH PRESS

Sewanee, Tennessee

THE DOWAGER'S CHIHUAHUA:

RELIGION BY THE SEAT OF YOUR PANTS

By The Rt. Rev. R. Heber Gooden

Copyright © 1993 by University of the South Press

Reprinted February 1994

The University of the South Press

735 University Avenue

Sewanee, TN 37383-1000

ISBN 0-918-769-17-5

Rarely are we given such a winsome picture of a long and remarkably diverse ministry as this work by Bishop Heber Gooden. It is so self-effacing and lightly handled that there is danger its depth and substance may go unnoticed. Even more important, in that unfathomable mystery of faith as gift, one can scarcely help but have one's own faith nurtured and encouraged by this story of unself-conscious confidence in the Christian Gospel.

In a day when much theology is written in a form virtually inaccessible to many church people, it is refreshing to read an account of a life through which a most effective ministry is easily discerned. Here is a unique blend of theological substance and hilarious humor frequently expressed in memorable one-line aphorisms, e.g. "a concrete mind: all mixed up and permanently set."

We owe Heber a great debt for his recovery of that most elusive of spirits, the reverent hilarity that is not only fitting and congruent with the Gospel, but is an indispensable dimension of its wholeness. Yet humor is rarely associated with church or with the Christian faith, so it is important to understand why and how it is not only appropriate, but urgently needed.

Those of us who have been privileged to know Bishop Gooden cannot help but smile when his name is mentioned. His humor is characteristic of him, and in remembering how we laughed we risk forgetting the serious commitments adumbrated by his stories and illustrations. Yet concentration on them runs the risk incumbent on any attempt to take humor seriously.

Humor is indeed a very serious subject, but one like Heisenberg's Principle of Indeterminacy: the very attempt to measure the sub-atomic realities interferes with the observation itself. Likewise, humor tends to be lost when one begins to analyze it in order to understand its nature and functions. Nevertheless, it is worthwhile to try to understand something of how and why this aspect of Heber's ministry is so important.

One of the many graceful functions of humor is its ability to bring us down to earth from unwarranted pretension and *hubris*. "Angels are said to fly because they take themselves so lightly." Another of his stories illustrates how the occasional but universal uppityness of children can be confronted with candor and grace by humor. Heber's first wife was Spanish of Basque extraction. His two adolescent sons were once showing little respect for their mother and Heber reminded them that they were "half-Basque sons of a bishop."

Heber has given us some understanding of another deeper and more valuable function of humor as expressed in the observation by the Anglican poet and playwright, Christopher Fry: "Comedy is an escape, not from truth but from despair, a narrow escape into faith." On numerous occasions in the House of Bishops, when things were quite tense and frustrating, Bishop Heber Gooden has gotten up and told one of his inimitable stories and had the House in tumultuous laughter. This comic relief provided an escape from despair—not from truth—as we returned to our tasks with a confidence and patience that had been clouded by frustrations.

A certain grimness in some distortions of Christianity carries the name Pelagianism. This ancient and perennial heresy, the enemy of laughter and joy, is the religious equivalent of nagging. Its adherents and victims are characterized by the absence of humor and it has about it a Promethean tragic seriousness of gnostic proportions that leads us to see our bodies and our time as prisons against which we must contend.

In contrast, the comic figure in literature echoes something akin to the messages of the Incarnation: that Christ took on our flesh and lived in the dimension of our time. His body was no prison and his time was no curse. The comic figure does not rail against these realities nor whine over their limitations. What was good enough for God in Christ is good enough for us to live this life under these conditions of body and time.

Humor in Scripture has been a most elusive reality and nowhere brought to our attention with greater clarity than by the actor Alec McCowan delivering Mark's Gospel in simple, straightforward King James diction with no props but a table and a glass of water. His presentation was serious and not irreverent, a plain delivery of the shortest of Gospels. Yet much to my surprise and delight, the audience (one had to buy tickets to a Broadway theater) on numerous occasions burst out in spontaneous laughter, something I had never heard when it was read in church. (In 1978 when Mr. McCowan delivered this at the Lambeth Conference of Bishops in Canterbury, England, the Bishops laughed even more enthusiastically than did the New York audiences.)

There is something surprisingly humorous in Scripture (Mark 10:35-41 was heard with especially great laughter) that is lost to most of us. Humor is notoriously difficult to translate and what is not lost by guilt and grimness is too easily lost as the story has passed from Aramaic through Greek and Latin, to King James' English, to our own day.

This concentration on one aspect of Bishop Gooden's life and ministry, his matchless sense of humor, should not obscure from us the total seriousness of his exemplary witness and faithfulness as missionary, pastor, teacher, dean, and bishop. His book, his life and ministry, recover and preserve for us something very precious of the Christian faith and indicates why so many of us revere and love him.

THE RT. REV. C. FITZSIMONS ALLISON
Bishop of South Carolina (Retired)

On his 80th anniversary my father's little grand-daughter, Ann, said, "Grandpa, you are now an octogeranium." I recently became that. I am much closer to "On Golden Pond" than to "The Blue Lagoon." My chances of dying of old age are getting better all the time.

But before I do that I would like to write a book that you may never see because it may never be published. Regardless of that, I feel that I must do it, not because my friends say, "You should write a book," but because this book has been slowly incubating in me for about seven decades. It is the fruit of years of ministry as a pastor to people of all kinds and conditions in many different countries that I am willing to share with any-one who is interested.

My ministry began in Spain where I studied as a graduate student at the University of Madrid on a fellowship in 1934–35. While there, I was Honorary Assistant Chaplain to the British Embassy Church. Honorary meant non-stipendiary, a fancy word signify-ing that I received no pay for my part-time service.

It has been alleged that a clergyman is a prime ex-ample of the fact that virtue does not pay. However, I have always enjoyed my work regardless of that.

While in Madrid, I stayed as a paying guest with a Spanish family. Fortunately, they were not interested in learning English. I wanted to learn Spanish because I had a job waiting for me in Cuba at the end of 1935.

At times my head would almost burst with the strain of hearing nothing but Spanish except on Sunday morning at St. George's Chapel. Sometimes I would go to the park to relax. But even the little children in Spain speak Spanish. If they could, certainly I could. However, everyone spoke so fast. It wasn't until a few months later that all of Spain began to slow down and it was easier for me to understand.

During my stay the civil war broke out. Spain became a battleground for the fascists and the communists to try out their weapons—a sort of spring practice for World War II.

Often, on my way to the library a strident voice would cry out to me, "Manos arriba!" "Hands up!" Even though I had books in my hands I had to walk with my hands up. Going to the library became a chore. Also, it was unsettling to have to dive under the table in our apartment while soldiers were firing their machine guns up the side of our building in an attempt to kill a sniper on the roof while we were at dinner.

The members of my Spanish "familia" and my classmates often would discuss questions or concerns, some of which were of a theological nature without their being aware of it. This book will deal with those questions.

I do not claim to be a theologian nor probably do you. We often think theologically whether we are aware of it or not. Some people are inclined to scoff at theology as obsolete and irrelevant. It is no more out of date than God. Yes, people may laugh at those medieval theologians who once argued heatedly about how many angels could dance on the head of a pin. A similar question might be today, "How many immaterial ideas and thoughts could be conceived or generated, or let's say dance, on a tiny bit of material substance or nerve tissue called gray matter?" Some of the most basic, important questions or concerns are of a theological nature, such as "Why is there anything at all?" "Where did I come from?" "What am I?" "Why am I here?" "Where am I going?" Democracy has theological roots. I will refer to these later.

A Welsh astronomer was quoted in a national weekly as follows: "To claim that life evolved from the random shuffling of amino acids is like saying that a tornado blowing through a junkyard accidentally produced a jumbo jet." Indeed, I wonder if you can be logical without being theological. If your brain evolved accidentally from an unreasoning source, how could you trust your thoughts? Is it reasonable to use reason to prove that reason is unreasonable or reasonable, for that matter.

In my 28 years as Bishop of the Episcopal Church in Latin America, I helped found a number of schools, some of them going from kindergarten through the 12th grade. An older student once said to me, in Spanish, "Señor Obispo, creo solamente en lo que se puede probar científicamente." ("Bishop, I believe only in that which can be proved scientifically.") "Does your mother love you?" I replied. "But of course!" said he. "Prove it scientifically," I answered. Some of the most important things in life are not subject to scientific analysis, including the scientist's wife and children. You have to have faith; you have to believe. You can't live without these. Faith and belief are inescapable. We are all believers even though we may not believe alike.

Before dealing further with the necessity or need to believe, I would say a word in passing about those angels. If you choose not to believe in their existence because you have never seen one or because it is "unscientific" to believe in their existence, that is your belief. It is an opinion to which you are entitled and which you cannot prove or disprove. I would not rule out the possibility of the presence of those spiritual beings somewhere in this vast universe. It is said that angels fly because they take themselves lightly. Perhaps we should lighten up in our own thinking and avoid the possibility of having our concrete minds all mixed up and permanently set.

R. Heber Gooden

ACKNOWLEDGMENTS

I acknowledge with heartfelt thanks the following persons who helped produce the manuscript of this book: approximately 20,000 people of various cultures, races, and ages, among whom I had the privilege and pleasure of working during the 58 years of my ministry in 15 countries, most of them in Latin America.

I am also grateful to those who took the trouble to read my manuscript and to make helpful suggestions: Bishop FitzSimons Allison, my mentor, who has done me the honor of writing the foreword.

I thankfully acknowledge the following whom I will list in alphabetical order: my sister, Muriel Badger; Canon Walter Baer; my sister and brother-in-law, Frances and Sterling Beckwith; my nephew, Herbert Beckwith; the Very Rev. Dale Coleman; my brother and sister-in-law, Bob and Pat Gooden; my deceased wife, Elena Gooden; our sons, Reginald Heber Gooden, Jr., and Richard Gooden; and my present wife, Sandra. I thank Bob Harwell, editor of the diocesan newspaper of Western Louisiana, *ALIVE*; Robert Powers; Dylis and Tom Wilson; and Bishop Robert Witcher. Jean Lanier transcribed my tapes and put them on the word processor. Her husband, Jesse, made numerous copies for me.

CONTENTS

THE DOWAGER'S CHIHUAHUA:
Religion by the Seat of Your Pants

There is a piddle which runs through the village of Wyre. For hundreds of years it has turned the wheel that grinds the wheat that makes the bread for the people to eat. I was told that 'piddle' was an old English word for stream.

There is also a stone church that was built in the time of the Normans some 900 years ago. On the floor of the church are two marble slabs marking the graves of the Norman knight and his lady who gave the money to build that beautiful little church.

Near that building is a convent where nuns in white habits prayed and also ministered to the spiritual needs of the neighborhood and tended the sick. The name still exists. White Ladies' Ashton is in the area of Flyford Flaven and Upton Snodsbury in the County of Worcestershire.

I had the privilege of preaching in that old church that was so small that I could almost have taken up the offering from the pulpit. The nave was packed and the people sang loudly and fervently. In my 13 years to date as a clergyman, I didn't believe I could have chosen a better place for Sunday worship than there with those hearty farmer folk who greeted me so warmly at the church door. I even appeared on the first page of the *Wyre Gazette* as the first American bishop to visit that church in 900 years and to sign the prayer books and hymnals of some of the children.

On my return to Lambeth Palace, the palace of the Archbishop of Canterbury, to join the hundreds of Anglican Bishops who were there for the Lambeth

Conference in July of 1948, some of my colleagues were standing in the courtyard telling what they had done over the weekend. They asked me what I had done. When I told them that I had preached in the church at Wyre Piddle, between Flyford Flaven and Upton Snodsbury near White Ladies' Ashton in Worcestershire, they claimed I had made that up!

With some exceptions, most of what you read in this book actually happened to me. For me, God is the bottom line. There is a spiritual or theological basis or meaning for most of what happens to us—even in the episodes of the dowager's Chihuahua that will appear later in this book. As I write some of this in a side-opening notebook in the airport or wherever the muse comes to me, I wonder what title to give it: "God is the bottom line;" or "You can't be logical without being theological;" or "Living is believing;" or "Why put a tiger in your tank when you have the same old unregenerate jackass behind the wheel?;" or "The Dowager's Chihuahua."

MY MOMMA AND DADDY AREN'T MARRIED

Back in 1939, soon after I became the Dean of Holy
Trinity Cathedral in Havana, Cuba, my wife and I were
getting up from the customary siesta when some early
callers knocked at our door. Our two-and-a-half year-
old son, Reggie, got there before we could and we heard
him say, "My momma and daddy aren't married."
"How do you know that?" they asked. "I know so
because I've been to Aunt Eugenia's wedding and Aunt
Stella's wedding, but I haven't been to my momma's
and daddy's wedding." He got his facts right, but he
drew the wrong conclusion. How can you prove to a
two-and-a-half year-old child that his or her parents are
married, especially since he wasn't there? You can say,
"Ask your Uncle Bob." But that would be hearsay, or
you could show him the marriage license, but remember, he can't read yet. You've got to believe; you have to
have faith. All through life we live by faith. We are all
believers, even though we don't always believe alike.

By faith the farmer sows his fields. By faith a husband
takes a wife and with probably more faith a wife takes a
husband. By faith you get into a taxi and, especially if
you are in Mexico City or Valencia, it takes a lot of faith
because the drivers seem to be full of bullfighter blood.
By faith you cross the street. The banker lives by faith.
He calls it credit. The agnostic might say, "I refuse to
believe, at least for now." But the agnostic is a person
who has both feet planted in mid-air. Sooner or later he
or she has to come down and make a decision one way
or the other.

An old West Indian woman once said to me in

Panama, "Bishop, if you don't got faith your prayers don't got no action." The scientist is a believer. Science is based on the belief or hypothesis that the universe is amenable to thought, that it is law-abiding and consistent. Obviously, faith or belief is not solely a religious concern. The atheist is often considered to be an unbeliever but he or she is really a fantastic believer. It takes faith to be a scientist. It takes faith to get married. It takes faith to pray. It takes faith to believe that God created the universe out of nothing. It takes enormously more faith to believe that from blind, inanimate, pre-existent incandescent hydrogen gas there evolved, quite by accident, the universe, intelligence, love, beauty, justice, truth, science, religion, art—all these from that original pre-existent mass of unthinking, lifeless, purposeless, formless, meaningless, superheated hydrogen gas, a belief that I prefer to call the hot-air theory. In our choice between God and no-God we are choosing between ultimate meaning and purpose or ultimate meaninglessness and absurdity.

We live in a world that science had made too small for small people. I'm not downgrading science. Who wouldn't rather have a washing machine than a washboard? Science has and can do much toward making a better world for us. It has achieved the dream of the ancient alchemist: to transmute lead into gold simply by removing from the lead atom three protons, three electrons, and eight neutrons at a cost of about one million dollars per troy ounce.

We can be grateful for the blessings of science, but whether science destroys the human race or offers us a happier, healthier life does not depend on science; it depends on the spiritual condition of the minds and souls of people. What we need today, as always, is that divine alchemy of the grace of God that alone can transmute the selfishness in the human heart to love of God and neighbor. If we can't sing, "Glory to God in the highest," there will be no "peace on earth, good will toward men." I like to say, "Why put a tiger in your tank if you've got the same old unregenerate jackass behind the wheel?" Therefore, to claim that it doesn't make any difference what you believe as long as you act all right is like saying that it doesn't make any difference what you eat or drink as long as you keep healthy.

R. Heber Gooden

One morning I boarded the Panama Railroad in Balboa, Canal Zone, on the Pacific side of the Isthmus of Panama, to go to Cristobal on the Atlantic side, a distance of approximately 50 miles. The coach was almost full. I sat next to a young man in military uniform who said to me, "Father, I would like to discuss religion with you but don't want to upset your faith." I said, "Well, you go right ahead and say whatever you want." He said, "Father, I'm an atheist. I don't believe in God." "When I was your age I was an atheist too, for a while. What are your reasons for being one?" He gave me the usual ones. I replied, "Are those the only reasons you have for being an atheist?" "Yes." "I'll give you a few more reasons." This put him in a more receptive frame of mind. It turned out that his atheism was not so much a matter of cold logic as cold feet, and he confessed that there were things in his life that he would have to change if he let God in, and he wasn't quite ready for that. Like St. Augustine before his conversion, he was saying "Five more minutes, Lord; five more minutes."

Dr. Hector J. Ritey, psychoanalyst and former medical director of the Metropolitan Center for Mental Health, has this to say about the atheist in his book, *The Human Kingdom.* "The denial of God is the climax of refusing to look at life." He goes on to explain that atheism is the rejection of the father image in an effort to escape from the responsibilities and realities of life into the irresponsibility and security of life before birth. Atheism is not always a sign of intellectual acumen, but of emotional immaturity.

In our choice between God or no-God, between ultimate meaning or ultimate meaninglessness, we have to decide one way or the other. There is a healthy agnosticism even in the Jewish and Christian faiths, as the Bible clearly discloses. But you cannot make up your mind not to make up your mind about the origin and meaning and destiny of life. This is what is involved in the decision between God and no-God.

The materialist believes that the only real things are those than can be weighed and measured, bought and sold. Materialism could be described as the "dog philosophy"—"What you can smell is. What you can't smell isn't." And there are many practicing materialists who would not admit the fact that they do not believe in God. They say, "Yes, we believe in God," and yet they feel like crossing themselves every time they pass the bank, and their spirits rise and fall with the Dow Jones average.

I will conclude this with a story that comes from World War II. A young navy pilot had made a number of mistakes such as bumping into planes on the flight deck. He was afraid that his superiors would soon give him some position other than flying. One morning, out in the Pacific the Japanese planes attacked and our pilots took off in defense. He made a perfect take-off, shot down two Japanese planes, and then made a perfect landing. He was very pleased with himself. He jumped out of his plane and ran over to an officer in a white uniform whose back was turned to him. He slapped him on the back saying, "This time I didn't make any mistakes. I made a perfect take-off. I shot down two Japanese planes and made a perfect landing." The officer turned around and said to him, "Ah so, but you make one mistake." It is a mistake to assume that we don't need to believe; that all beliefs are the same; that we don't owe anything to God; that morality and democracy don't have any religious foundations. It is a mistake to assume that we don't need God. The atheist has been aptly described as a person with no invisible means of support.

R. Heber Gooden

It is true but not always helpful. There are religious truths or beliefs and scientific truths or beliefs. One of the truths of science is stated in Albert Einstein's formula: "Energy equals mass times the speed of light squared." I presume that this is true throughout the universe and has always been true. However, when a husband is inside or outside the delivery room while his wife is in labor, does he comfort himself or help her by saying, "Energy equals mass times the speed of light squared?" And when we are at the graveside of a loved one does it console us to remember that, "Energy equals mass times the speed of light squared." It is true, but who cares that, "Energy equals mass times the speed of light squared?" What we want to know then is, does God care?

Many religious people believe that God does care, and Christians believe that God has revealed that truth to us through the love manifested in Jesus Christ—love as humble as His birth in a Bethlehem stable, as self-sacrificing and outreaching as His death on that Cross on Calvary, as victorious as the empty tomb at Jerusalem, and as powerful as Pentecost transforming the lives of millions upon millions of people. His living presence enables them to hope.

There are four very important questions that we humans ask ourselves, consciously or perhaps unknowingly, and what we believe the answers are as vital to our lives. The questions are: "Where did I come from?" "What am I?" "Why am I here?" and "Where am I going?" Every religion and philosophy attempts to give the answer to these questions.

There is the story about a lion who was walking in the jungle and to every creature he said, "Who is the king of the beasts?" They trembled and said, "You are." Finally, he came to an elephant. He looked up at the elephant and asked him, "Who is the king of the beasts?" The elephant paid no attention. He asked him again. The elephant lowered his trunk, picked up the lion, twirled him around his head and threw him into a thicket. Finally the lion emerged, dusting himself off with his paws, and said, 'Well, you didn't have to go to all that trouble just because you didn't know the answer."

I believe that the Christian faith gives us the fullest and best answers to these questions.

WHY IS THERE ANYTHING AT ALL?

Years ago my son, Dick, then only four years old, asked me this question, and I could think of only one answer: "Because God made it." That is still my answer. Of course, this is a belief shared by many—Jew and Gentile alike, and others. Still, there are those who say that the universe has always existed. Then we could ask, "Why has there always existed anything at all?" If the universe always existed, why is there any radioactivity left? Why hasn't it all died out by now? Others say it happened quite by accident 20 billion years ago as a result of a gigantic primordial explosion. They seem to shy away from the belief that it was created. Can a picture paint itself if the brush has a long enough handle? Shakespeare ate meat and potatoes, but did they write his plays? Sir Alexander Fleming discovered penicillin. It certainly wasn't the other way around. For me and probably for you, the most logical belief is found in the Bible—"In the beginning God..." Because He is, we are! He made us in His image. That does not mean that we are pint-sized editions of God. It means that He has given us an awareness of Himself, our Creator, and the freedom to love Him and serve Him and our neighbor or to ignore them.

There is a poem by a well-known author whose name is Anonymous, or "Anon" for short. It is entitled "Darwin's Mistake:

> *Three monkeys sat in a coconut tree,*
> *discussing things as they are said to be.*
> *Said one to the others, "Now listen, you two,*
> *there's a certain rumor that just can't be true.*

That man descended from our noble race.
The very idea is a disgrace!
No monkey ever deserted his wife,
starved her babies and ruined her life.
And there's another thing a monkey wouldn't do;
go out at night and get in a stew.
And use a club or a knife
to take some other monkey's life!
Yes, man descended, the ornery cuss.
But brother, he didn't descend from us!

Humans are free to be worse than they are. Monkeys are not. No animal can be worse than he or she is. Take, for example, a crocodile. If a crocodile eats a missionary or two, he is not a bad crocodile. If he eats a drug pusher, he is not a good crocodile. He is just your ordinary, run-of-the-mill, full-bodied, red-blooded, normal, ipso facto crocodile, doing what comes naturally. A human can choose to live on a sub-human level; he can make a monkey or an ass of himself. Evolution does not mean that there is no significant difference between humans and all the other creatures.

In addition to God's gift of freedom that we spoke of, we have what might be called reflexive consciousness. Some animals know; but we are the only ones that know we know. God, in His love, gave us grace and made us aware not only of ourselves, but of Him. He gave us freedom and responsibility and the right to choose. Indeed, in this and in other ways, we are different from those three monkeys in the coconut tree.

I heard this recently, as an attention grabber or attention getter. Perhaps the greatest gift to humanity is motherhood. You probably think you have or had the best mother in all the world. I hope you do. I believe that about my mother. I owe my life to her in more ways than one.

When my father was a student at Berkeley Divinity School in Middletown, Connecticut, he also was organist and choir director at an Episcopal Church in Hartford where a young lady named Alice sang in the choir. I am told that one evening he reprimanded the choir. Alice apparently was offended by that and did not come to the choir or to a rehearsal for perhaps two weeks. My father went to call on her. I don't know what he said but it must have been effective because they became engaged. Some years later my future mother and her husband moved to Long Beach, California, where he was rector of St. Luke's Church and where I was born in the rectory. There was an epidemic of measles and whooping cough in 1910 and my oldest sister brought these home from school when I was about two weeks old. I caught both of them. It is said that my mother nursed me day and night and bathed me in alcohol to keep my fever down. I was so close to death that they thought I should be baptized right away before I died.

My godmother had a little white coffin made for me as a kind of going away gift. Some years later as I watched my mother comb her waist-long hair I said, "Mother, where did you get that white box that you keep things in on your dresser?" She embraced me and said, "Heber, that is a gift from your godmother. It was a coffin, and when I look at it I thank God that you have outgrown it." I thank God for the love of a mother who made this happen. One thing I know: I'll never outgrow my love and appreciation for my mother!

When my brother, three sisters, and I were children, we always had prayers after breakfast. Usually my father conducted them. They would consist of a bible reading followed by prayer and then we would go to the living room where we gathered around the piano where my father played a familiar hymn. When father was absent mother would lead us in the prayer and accompany us at the piano singing along with us such hymns as:

> *New every morning is the love*
> *our wakening and uprising prove;*
> *through sleep and darkness safely brought,*
> *restored to life and power and thought.*
> *New mercies each returning day,*
> *around us hover while we pray;*
> *new perils past, new sins forgiven,*
> *new thoughts of God, new hopes of heaven.*

As I sang, I looked at her and thought, "She is as close to heaven as I can get in this world." Then we children, fortified with vitamin "R," would walk to grammar school—the 24th Street Public School, about a mile away in the suburbs of Los Angeles. Vitamin "R" is the most important of all the vitamins; it is the "religious" vitamin without which children grow up to be morally rachitic and spiritually retarded.

When I was a student at the University of Madrid, I traveled to Seville in southern Spain to see the "Pasos de Semana Santa"—the religious processions for Holy Week. Seville was noted for the Holy Week processions. There were floats carried by stevedores who were concealed beneath with draperies. The floats portrayed the Last Supper, the Crucifixion, and other episodes of Holy Week. But the float that received the most respect and reverence was the one with the Blessed Virgin Mary.

In those days there was much communism and atheism in Spain, especially among the working classes. As the Blessed Virgin Mary went by all talking ceased. The men removed their hats and some even crossed themselves. There was a saying in Spain, "No creo en Dios, pero la Virgen es Su Madre," that means, "I don't believe in God, but the Virgin is His mother." For most people, the love of God is more apparent in motherhood than anywhere else.

When I left my Christian home to enter Stanford University in 1927, I came to experience what has been described as "the first wild seeds of religious doubt." Some of the students and even some of the professors claimed to be atheists. This shook my faith, but it turned out to be fruitful in my case because it made me rethink my faith, which made it become more relevant to me.

While I was searching, I reluctantly said to my father, then the headmaster of my former prep school, "I believe in evolution." "So do I," he replied. This came as a pleasant relief to me, as I did not realize then that the main difference between a father and a son is 20 or more years of experience. Yes, you can believe in God and evolution at the same time, and you don't have to choose between science and religion. They complement one another; we need them both. That science can now accurately calculate the age of rocks does not do away with the "Rock of Ages."

Evolution without God is nothing more than biological survival through adaptation to one's environment. If that is all there is then the intestinal parasite and the cockroach are as advanced as we are. Materialism lets us down; a violin solo is not simply sound vibrations caused by rubbing a horse's tail over the entrails of an ex-cat stretched out on pieces of a dead tree. There must be more to life than mere physical survival. Our faith tells us that human life is more than what happens between two dates on a tombstone. Some ancient philosophers and theologians considered the possibility of evolution in creation and as a spiritual purpose involved in the whole of creation. St. Paul writes in the eighth chapter of his letter to the Romans: "Despite all the evidence to the contrary such as suffering, sickness, hatred, evil, nothing could thwart God's purpose or separate us from the love of God revealed through Jesus Christ."

Elsewhere, we will write about why bad things happen to good people and good things happen to bad people. The late Ayatollah Khomeini said, "We must forgive our enemies but only after they are hanged." Jesus said, "Love your enemies." Who's right? A Nobel Prize winner in physics, Arthur Compton, wrote: "Science has made Christianity indispensable." A biologist allegedly crossed a parrot with a tiger. When asked about the result he replied, "I don't know, but when that thing talks, I listen!" The H-Bomb is saying, "Be one or none." If we haven't had World War III already, it may be that we realize that in such a war we would run out of people before we ran out of ammunition. I believe that we have reached a point in human history where the alternative to love of God and neighbor is suicide. I believe that our best hope for oneness is in Christ. It takes faith to believe this. It takes faith to believe in the love of God, especially if you have cancer, for example.

You can't live without believing. The most important decisions in life are the choice of a vocation and the choice of a spouse. Both choices are made on inadequate grounds. You are not qualified to make these choices unless you have had the experience, and you can't have the experience unless you've made the choice. You've got to commit yourself. Much of life is like a stained glass window—you can't appreciate it from outside the church. You have to go inside.

R. Heber Gooden

My mother told me, "Don't go into the water until you have learned how to swim." This is an old joke that was told about the year 425 B.C. by the Greek statesman and philosopher Pericles. We can't learn how to swim without getting wet. We learn by experience, by putting our faith into practice. It isn't enough to say "I believe that God exists." We must commit ourselves to Him, to be in communication with God to believe in Him.

I know a clergyman who when he was 24 years old— a deacon still wet behind his ecclesiastical ears—made one of his first pastoral calls. He visited a recently bereaved dowager to extend his condolences. A maid ushered him into a dimly lighted parlor from the bright sunshine. He sat down in a black overstuffed chair and felt something crunch beneath him. To his dismay, it was a black Chihuahua puppy. He had crushed the life out of it! He heard footsteps coming down the stairway. He said to himself, "I killed her pet puppy. If I hand it to her she may die of a heart attack the way her husband did last week. What did I learn in the seminary about how to cope with this situation? What did pastoral theology say about what do you do when you sit on the dowager's Chihuahua?" Not one word. He had to do something, one way or the other. In this case he put the little dog in his pocket, made a short visit and buried the creature in his garden. Burying the puppy was not enough. The morning paper contained a picture of him and the offer of a reward for his return. The young deacon had to make restitution. The best way he could do this was to search in the pet shops for a puppy that resembled the one he had killed. After finding one, he put it in a shoe box with air holes in it and took it to the lady with the explanation that he heard her dog had strayed and here was one that looked like the picture in the newspaper. The "restitution" cost him one-fourth of his meager monthly salary, but was worth it to see the delighted face of the dowager as she clasped the little creature to her bosom.

Never again did that clergyman sit down before taking a good look. We do learn from experience.

In the Episcopal Home in Alhambra, where I lived for awhile, the average age is 82. There are more years of experience in that relatively small area than perhaps in a square mile of the rest of the city. The residents of that home have experienced joy and sorrow, pleasure and pain, and the death, not of just one loved one but of many loved ones, some of them even their own grand-children. More than that, most of them are experiencing the frustration of a mind that says "Go, go," and a body that says, "No, no." That is experience. There is a Spanish proverb that says, "Si la juventud supiera y la vejez pudiera." "If youth only knew, and old age could only do." These people have learned how to put their faith to work. They have found that the love that will not let them go will not let them down. They have trusted in Him and the trust has not been in vain. They ventured into the water and learned how to swim.

A woman once said to her pastor, "Christianity has been in the world a long time, but look at the mess the world is in." Just then her son came running up to her covered with mud from making mud-pies. The clergy-man replied, "Water has been in the world a long time but just look at your son." Gilbert K. Chesterton put it this way, "Christianity has not been tried and found wanting, it has been found wanting where it has not been sincerely tried."

I close with a story about my grand-nephew who said, "Grandma, will you still be alive when I'm in the third grade?" He was then in the second grade. Now he is in the fifth grade and his Grandma is still alive and well.

The important question for us is, will God still be alive in us? He will if we commit ourselves to Him. As we go through life, we will grow if He lives in us. Someone has said, "Our lives are God's gift to us; what we do with them is our gift to God."

The next three essays will deal with basic human needs: "We all want security." "We all want to be loved." "We all want to feel important and see meaning in our existence." The difference between people is not in what they want but in how they try to get it.

R. Heber Gooden

What a blessing to think that we could be completely secure from poverty, sickness, accident, and every unpleasant thing, as long as we live in this world and thereafter. This longing began perhaps long before we were born. When I am handed a crying infant at baptism, I can usually make it stop crying by holding it tight.

Security. We all want it. But how do we go about getting it? One of the commonest ways to meet this need is through material wealth. This is an acceptable symbol of security. It can be a cushion against the misfortunes and discomforts of life to a degree. If I am dying on a hot day, I appreciate having the air conditioner on. Health insurance is a form of security also. But as we know, even the best insurance is like those hospital gowns: every time you turn around you find something that is not covered. Inflation can steal your money from a safe without opening the door. Technology can make us more secure, but it can keep us alive even after our brain is dead, and that is a growing concern for our older people. Politics can help, but we know that often politicians promise us pie-in-the-sky with our own dough. We believe that national defense should be strong. A balanced budget, democratic freedom, economic development, and international cooperation, all contribute to security. However, though we have always longed for security, it cannot be found in things alone or in this world only. Our true security is in God's hands and the knowledge that he is our strength and lasting hope.

A little child said this in a bed-time prayer, "O God, please keep Mama and Daddy and my sisters and brothers; and God, please look after yourself, too, because if anything bad should happen to you, we'd all be sunk." Security has its spiritual basis and when we know this we begin to feel secure inside where it counts. "The Lord shall preserve thy going out and thy coming in from this day forth and forevermore." Therefore, we find in our Christian faith the fulfillment of one of humanity's greatest needs. This is summed up in that familiar hymn, "O God, our help in ages past, our hope for years to come, our shelter from the stormy blast, and our eternal home."

R. Heber Gooden

We all have a need for love. How true it is that the child who is never an armful can grow up to become a handful. Everyone needs to be loved, not just with possessive and sentimental love. That love is immature, like puppy love which never builds homes but only doghouses. We never have lived and we never will be able to live by bread alone. We seek the fulfillment of this basic need for love in various ways, through home and family and devoted service to those in need.

Some people have tried to satisfy this longing at a merely physical level, only to find that something is lacking because love is far more than physical. The physical part is enhanced and dignified by the spiritual, and thus love becomes sacramental as it is referred to in the marriage service in the Book of Common Prayer, a union between body and soul. It was Zsa Zsa Gabor who said, "The only thing Conrad Hilton and I had in common was his money." God made both body and soul, and just as a home is more than a house and a person is more than a body, so love must have its spiritual nature. When we see this truth, we realize that love is of God; an undeserved, unmerited gift that He is willing to bestow on all of his children without exception. All other loves must fade. Death inevitably separates us from our loved ones at least for a while. Only God's love can remain with us no matter where we go; His love enables and enhances human love in its manifold expressions.

How do we know that God is love? A Soviet scientist said, "I have searched the heavens with my telescope and found no trace of God." Did he expect to find God with a piece of curved glass? Can he find art in a dab of pigment? Or love in an equation? Those who seek God only in these things are looking in the wrong place. "The heavens declare the glory of God and the firmament showeth His handiwork." The famous astronomer Johannes Kepler, a friend of Galileo, once exclaimed as he examined the firmament through his telescope, "O God, I think thy thoughts after Thee." All of nature is sacramental for those with eyes to see the inward and spiritual grace and glory and power and wisdom and goodness of the Creator in the things that he has made.

Professor Stephen Hawking is widely regarded as the most brilliant theoretical scientist since Einstein. In his book, *A Brief History of Time*, Hawking states, "If we discover a complete theory (meaning a complete theory of the universe), it should in time be understandable in broad principle by everyone, not just a few scientists. Then we shall be able to take part in the discussion of the question, 'Why is it that we and the universe exist?' If we find the answer to that, it would be the ultimate triumph of human reason. For then we would know the mind of God."

Professor Hawking's phrase, "the mind of God," reminds me of a scene in Thornton Wilder's play, *Our Town*: a young person is telling a friend about a letter she had received with this unusual address:

> Grover's Corners, New Hampshire, U.S.A.,
> Western Hemisphere,
> World, Solar System,
> Universe, The Mind Of God.

I knew Mr. Wilder when I was a student at Berkeley

Divinity School at Yale in New Haven, Connecticut. His best known novel is *The Bridge of San Luis Rey*. He was a devout Christian whose belief in God was not only intellectual but existential. He experienced his faith, I believe, as I believe he also did, that we cannot know "the mind of God" by reason alone but through experience in which we respond to God's revelation in faith.

Science is also based on faith in the hypothesis that this is a universe and not a multi-verse that it is amenable to thought.

The fact that we exist is a sign of God's creative mind and also His love. The fact that we are even aware of Him and are able to communicate with Him in prayer and sacrament are signs of God's love for us. Whoever has experienced the joy of forgiven sin and the redemptive grace of God can never doubt the reality of God's love.

In Jesus we find the supreme manifestation of that love. It is our Lord who gave a friendly name to the Thinker behind the thought, the Person behind personality, the Judge behind the moral law. In the New Testament, we find the word "Father" appearing 275 times. The Gospel is the world's greatest love story. If we doubt the reality of God's love for us, this doubt does not necessarily have its roots in our intellect, but in our pride. Like the elder brother in the Prodigal Son, some people resent God's love and forgiveness so freely bestowed on sinners whom we have not forgiven. Like the Pharisees who criticized our Lord, they do not approve of the company God keeps. "How inconsiderate of Him to forgive our enemies and to love those whom we distrust and hate. God has no right to act so unilaterally in these matters. It's embarrassing!" And yet how well would we fare if God gave us what we actually deserved, if His justice were not tempered by mercy? No, it is not our intellect that makes us question God's love, but only our pride that separates us from God and neighbor. In the love of God that has been revealed to us through Christ, we know that we are loved forever. The person who responds to that love will know what it is to find a love that will not let us go.

The third of our basic needs and longings is to feel
significant or important. The wrong ways of fulfilling
this desire have resulted in more ulcers, hypertension,
heartaches, and wars than we might imagine. What
some people won't do for recognition is beyond belief!
If, for example, a man cannot be significant in an acceptable way, he may become Napoleon in some mental
hospital. A little boy once prayed, "Dear God, my Dad
thinks he's You. Please straighten him out." Fortunately,
most of us don't go to such extremes. Many, however,
settle for the rat race of status symbols. Keeping up with
the Joneses is symptomatic of the longing to be important and recognized. Some folk are like billboards,
flashy on the outside, but behind is a vacant lot of
emptiness, debts, and anxiety. The most important job
for any human being is to be one. Some of you may have
heard of "Steam Train Flanigan," the King of the Hobos.
At his coronation, he said these words: "To be is important. To be important is not."

We need a doctrine of man, or humanity, but what
shall it be? Are we merely animals? Do we have no
value in ourselves? Almost every day in the United
Nations, the delegates are deciding for or against some
doctrine of man. Whether we have world slavery or
world freedom, depends on the answer: "What are we?"
Our lasting worth and importance can be found in the
doctrine of man that claims we are children of God and
inheritors of eternal life. The warfare outside of us and
the conflicts inside struggle for meaning and significance. We can never be content with being only mem-

bers of a race, or a nation, or a class. Our restlessness is a divine restlessness that God has placed in our souls when He made us in His image and created us free persons with eternal value. When you find it difficult to love your neighbor, pray for him or her. Our neighbors are children of God worthy of our respect and of our love.

Finally, I read somewhere that when the Son of Man, on the night He was betrayed, knelt down to wash the feet of His disciples, a new revolutionary ethic was born. The time will come when we shall realize that it was not the clash of arms or the awesome blast of the nuclear bomb, but the tinkling of water poured into a basin in that upper room in Jerusalem that sounded the death knell to oppression and special privilege and all else that seeks to deprive people of their birthright as children of God, and strives to undermine their self-respect as free eternal souls. And thus, in my belief, Christianity meets these basic needs: security in the everlasting arms of God, life lived in the assurance of a love that will not let us go, and enduring significance and value as children of God and inheritors of the kingdom of heaven.

In the Preface of this book I said that Democracy has theological roots. You are familiar with the phrase, "Under God" in the pledge of allegiance to our flag. And on our money we read, "In God We Trust." Abraham Lincoln said, "We kneel to God or we bow to tyrants." This is historically true. George Washington said in his farewell address, "Of all the dispositions and habits which lead to political prosperity, religion and morality are the indispensable supports. In vain would that man claim the tribute of patriotism who had subverted these great pillars of human happiness, these firm props of the duties of men and citizens." The Brookings Institution, a well-known scholarly research organization, published an extensive study in 1985 in a book titled *Religion in American Political Life*. This study emphasizes the fact that secularism is providing an inadequate foundation for democracy in America. In it we read: "Human rights are rooted in the moral worth with which a loving Creator has endowed each human soul, and social authority is legitimized by making it amenable to transcendent moral value." In other words, the study rejects the argument that strict separation of Church and State is needed. And it goes on to say, "A society that excludes religion as something from which public life must be protected, is bound to foster the impression that religion is either harmful or irrelevant." Lastly it states: "From the beginnings of American history, religion and the practice of democracy have been closely intertwined."

It is true that we are a pluralistic society and therefore

we should not sponsor an official religion or official church. However, most Americans recognize that this nation is "Under God," although there are many different concepts of the nature of God, as you know.

I have heard that in Greece a tourist got into a rope basket which was tied by another rope in order to be pulled up the side of a steep cliff to gain access to a monastery. The tourist noticed that the rope was frayed and that it was a long way up and would, of course, be a long way down. He said to the monks, "How often do you change this rope?" They said, "Only when it breaks!" If we ignore or reject the fact that values must be transcendent, we are in danger of losing those values.

I mentioned in the Preface that I am not as young as I used to be. In fact, sometimes my friends wish to know how many prunes I would like in my martini. However, all jesting aside, there are advantages to being old. For example, I had the privilege and pleasure of attending a performance of a musical called "Lil Abner." I recall a song that goes like this:

> O happy day, when miracles take place,
> and scientists control the human race.
> O happy day, when in collective brains
> no individuality remains.
> We'll be a race of busy bees in happy honeycombs,
> so much of this, so much of that, for ears and eyes,
> so much of this, so much of that for toes and thighs.
> Pour in a pot, stir up a lot. That's the basic plan.
> What have you got? I'll tell you what.
> You've got a man-made man.

This is the danger that we are running into today. We forget that we are under God. The values that we accept and cherish, or ought to accept and cherish, are also "under God." In other words, they are transcendent. They are not man-made. We didn't vote them in and can't vote them out, even if we tried to. If we do, we are going to be in trouble. The Church and the synagogue and our educational institutions should become more aware of the religious foundations of democracy.

Towards the beginning of this book I said, "All through life we live by faith and we are all believers." Belief of some kind is inescapable.

Most people who believe in God engage in some form of prayer. Al Gahazi, the Moslem mystic, said, "If you don't have time for prayer you don't have time for God." Prayer is a uniquely human activity.

In response to His disciples' request, "Lord, teach us to pray," Jesus answered, "When you pray, say our Father." He gave us what is called "The Lord's Prayer:" a brief prayer that includes many of the elements of prayer: petition, intercession, thanks, penance, and communion. It begins with adoration.

In adoration we put ourselves into the presence of God to whom we are praying. The Lord's Prayer is not a "me first" prayer. Such as, for example, "Lord, be good to me, Christ make things easy for me, and deliver me from the necessity of having to do anything whatsoever. Lord, I have every intention of repenting before I die, but Lord please give me at least five minutes warning. Help my toothache to go away without having to trouble that poor busy dentist. Use me, even me, if only in an advisory capacity. When I must argue with a stubborn fool, keep him or her from being similarly occupied," and so on.

We may laugh at such prayers, they are exaggerations, and yet it's very easy to pray like that. I've done it often. Prayer is not telling God what to do. He already knows. It is not a "cop-out" for doing the things we can and should do with God's help. And prayer, as we said, is not self-centered. It is God-centered. However, in case you're worried, it is far better to pray foolishly than not to pray at all.

As we mature in prayer, our prayers will get to be more like our Lord's Prayer. In that prayer we ask God for bread, that's Petition, but only after we have praised Him; only after we have asked Him to reign in our hearts and in our world. Jesus said, "Seek ye first God, and His righteousness and all those other things will be added unto you." God is alive to us and we are alive to Him if we seek His presence and grace and guidance and loving companionship in worship and prayer. In as much as God is, and we are, there ought to be an ever-deepening relationship between the two of us.

God wants us to have conscious, voluntary fellowship with Him. St. Augustine said, "Thou hast made us for Thyself, O God, and our hearts are restless until they find their rest in Thee." He will not impose Himself on us. It takes two to pray. It takes God and us.

What is prayer? There are many definitions and many books have been written on this subject. I certainly haven't read all of them. For me, one of the best definitions that I can think of is, "Prayer is friendship with God." It is this friendship, companionship, or fellowship that keeps us from loneliness, from anxiety, and from shallowness. Recently I saw a bumper-sticker that read, "Why pray when you can worry?" That is a whimsical way of stating what we have just said. It is the kind of prayer that is friendship with God, frequent and regular, that nourishes our souls, gives us an increasingly Christian knowledge of God and of ourselves, and brings us purpose, peace, and hope. This kind of prayer is not an opiate. It is not an escape. It is a means of facing or coping with life realistically. It is living life at its best, and it is God's way of helping us to fulfill the chief purpose for which we were made. I think the Presbyterian catechism states it very well: "Our chief duty or purpose is to love God, to serve God, and to enjoy Him forever." That's worth trying.

People complain of disappointing experiences when they pray. Some people assume that they can become conscious of God anytime they want to, regardless of their mood or behavior. People who are superficial and selfish on their feet, cannot suddenly become a saint on their knees. That's not the way it works. There are some cases of instantaneous conversion, but I'm talking about ordinary folk like me. We must persevere. God gave us spiritual nature, and we can develop it with His grace if we keep at it. Some people criticize us for being what they call "anthropomorphic," or treating God as a king-size Mr. Jones or queen-size Ms. Jones. But tell me, is an impersonal, inanimate "'It" superior to the concept of a personal, wise, loving God who taught us to pray, "Our Father . . .?"

Jesus taught us to say, "Give us . . .," to God. But we must not limit ourselves to asking for ourselves. As we grow in prayer, we find that it is friendship with Him that is really desirable and needful. Jesus said, "Seek ye first God and His righteousness, and all these other things will be added unto you." He also said, "Nevertheless, not my will but thine be done." Therefore, we often end our prayer as Christians with the words, "through Jesus Christ our Lord," or "In Jesus' name." Which means that we do not presume that God needs to be told what He already knows or that we have to tell Him what to do. It means that we cannot expect Him to grant us anything whatsoever even if He thinks it happens to be contrary to what He thinks is best for us and for our world. God always hears our prayers and He always answers. As someone once said, "Sometimes He says yes, sometimes He says no, sometimes He says wait, but He never says perhaps."

I had a friend who used to frustrate me sometimes. He was in charge. Often, when I would try to get some advice from him, he was reluctant to give it to me. Once he said, "I'll tell you something, Heber, I'll give you a definite perhaps." Not very helpful.

R. Heber Gooden

There are many other kinds of prayers including Meditation and Thanksgiving. I would like to say just a few words about Intercessory Prayer.

"God help me" is a prayer of Petition. "God help my neighbor" is a prayer of Intercession. Someone has described a prayer of intercession as loving our neighbor on our knees. When praying for others it is helpful to try to imagine that particular person in the presence of God. Nobody knows what God looks like but we have reason to believe that He's there, that He can hear, and that He loves and will help. Don't ask God for the whole world in general when you are making your Intercessions, but select certain people whom you know to be sick and think of these people and their specific needs, physical and spiritual. Think of them as becoming whole and well. Pray for different people every day. Don't pray for a hundred people at once. You won't have time, and I don't think you will find it effective from your standpoint. These people often do get well, and when they get well how about thanking God for that? I've had people call me up after they got well and thank me because they got well. Of course, I know that it was God that healed them, but it's nice to know that there's one less person you have to pray for to get well because they are already well.

Sometimes people don't get well. They die. As a matter of fact, everybody does in time. Then what happens? God answered that prayer. My faith tells me that they are better off than before. I assume that's true, especially if they were suffering. We already know that

God loves those whom we love far more than we could possibly love them, infinitely more. Jesus taught us to pray for others. He said, "Pray for those who hate you." So when we pray for others, we ought to realize that we should be instruments of God, that we should be willing to help these people. Don't just leave it up to God and say, "All right God, I told you what to do, now just do it!" God will help them through us. And also when we make a habit of praying for others we ourselves become more sensitive to other people's needs and more under-standing and more willing to respond.

C. S. Lewis wrote, "Infinite wisdom does not need telling what is best, and infinite goodness needs no urging to do it." But neither does God need any of those other things that are done by finite agents. God can give us food without farmers and cooks. He can give us knowledge without teachers, books or schools, and health without physicians, nurses, and hospitals, and He can covert the heathen without any missionaries. Yes, He can do that. But, says C. S. Lewis, "He always allows soil and weather and animals, and the muscles and the minds and wills of people to cooperate in the execution of His will. And so it is with our prayers. God does not care more for the billions of stars and the billions of galaxies than He does for His children to whom He gives the miraculous ability and opportunity for prayer and friendship with Him."

I conclude by relating an experience that I had about six years ago. I was seated on a Continental Airlines plane. We were about to depart Houston for Shreveport after I had preached and confirmed in, I believe it was

St. Mark's Church, Beaumont. The flight attendant gave us the usual instructions regarding seat belts; where the exits are; and the smoking regulations. Then she added these words on her own: "Those found smoking in the aisles will kindly be asked to step outside." I wonder what happened to that woman? We applauded, laughed, even the smokers enjoyed that one. Nobody wants to step outside at 30,000 feet. Would you? To say the least, it's not very healthful.

However, when we break our contact with our Creator by neglecting our prayers and other means of spiritual growth, we are placing ourselves in an environment for which God never created us. God made us for fellowship with Him in this world and in that larger life beyond the grave. We are the only creatures that we know of, on this planet at least, who are capable of fellowship with Him in prayer and worship. Therefore, the neglect of prayer is hazardous to our spiritual health.

R. Heber Gooden

Jesus asked this question of his disciples at Ceasarea Philippi. We read about this in St. Matthew, Chapter 16, verses 13–17. He asked "Who do men say that the Son of Man is? (meaning the Messiah)." And they said, "Some say John the Baptist, others say Elija, others Jeremiah, or one of the prophets." He said to them, "But who do you say that I am?" And Simon Peter replied, "You are the Christ, the Son of the living God." And Jesus answered him saying, "Blessed are you, Simon, Son of Jonah, for flesh and blood has not revealed this to you, but my Father who is in heaven."

Today, as then, people give a variety of responses: "A great prophet; the greatest teacher or person that ever lived; but not Christ, not the Son of the living God. He didn't claim that for himself, the Church claimed that," and so on and so on.

It is alleged that a Japanese freighter sank in the Mississippi River with a full cargo of yo-yos. It sank forty times! The opinions that we have just heard have been bobbing up and down throughout the centuries. And these statements which we have just quoted from some people about the person of our Lord constitute an ancient heresy known as Arianism which was condemned at the First Council of Nicea in A.D. 325. The Nicene Creed states: "We believe in one God, in one Lord Jesus Christ, eternally begotten Son of God, Very God of Very God, being of one substance with the Father, by whom all things are made." Arias preached a half-truth. Most heresies are half-truths. They contain both truth and error. He said that Jesus was like God.

For him Jesus was God's look-a-like, but not the eternal Son of God, true God of true God.

The Good News is that Jesus is more than a prophet, more than the greatest teacher or person that ever lived. Salvation does not come from a book, or from the law, or from a great human example, such as God's look-a-like. It comes through the grace of God through Christ. Those who claim that they don't need grace belong to another heretical sect, which is very popular today. It is known as Pelagianism. "I can do it by myself, I can quit drinking all by myself. I don't need any help from anybody." Saint Paul declared, "Thanks be to God, who has given us the victory through our Lord Jesus Christ." Nevertheless, some of the old heresies still come and go, bobbing up and down like those yo-yos.

Some who do not believe what the disciples believed about Jesus and what Jesus said about Himself, contradict themselves. They say, "He's the greatest teacher that ever lived but he didn't really know who he was. He was meek and mild, and he never meddled in politics or business. The Church shouldn't do that either." You've heard that. Nevertheless, Jesus was crucified, not because he said, "Consider the lilies of the field, how they grow, but, behold, the thieves in the Temple, how they steal." That's what got him into trouble. They agreed that Jesus could not be God Incarnate, because that would be impossible.

When Adam and Eve were in the Garden of Eden naming the animals, (this is not in the Bible), they watched a hippopotamus come lumbering by. Eve said to Adam, "Let's call him hippopotamus." "Why?" said Adam. "Because he looks more like a hippopotamus than anything we've seen yet." Eve had an open mind. She was willing to accept something that looked as if it could not be, but she accepted it simply because it was. People, then and now, are quick to put ready-made labels on everything. They only consider as real something that they have already heard about and believed in or think to be credible; something they can fit into existing categories. For them, nothing can happen for the first time. That rules out Creation. As a matter of fact, it rules out us.

Furthermore, people who make conjectures about Jesus which are contrary to what He taught about Himself, or what His disciples taught about Him or believed about Him, are not really looking at Jesus. When Sir Isaac Newton stated the law of gravitation, he had almost no followers in his day, not even among his peers. They could not believe this law existed because it was in conflict with "the law of the concrete mind: all mixed up and permanently set," as I said before. Christopher Columbus had trouble with the law of the concrete mind. People said, "Chris, you can't do it. If you sail out there far enough you are going to fall off the ocean." Some who declined to accept Jesus Christ as Lord and Savior, or who refused to believe that God was and is in Christ, reconciling the world to Himself, claim that this would be a miracle and miracles don't happen.

Miracles could well be described as "acts of God." The back of, let us say, a steamship ticket enumerates many acts of God. If you ever plan to travel on a ship, don't look at the back of the ticket, because it tells you all the acts of God that can happen, for which the company is not responsible. They don't even have to take you where you're going!

There are some acts of God which I think are debatable and which are open to litigation, but there are other acts of God which we take for granted. We find a number of them in the Thanksgiving Prayer in *The Book of Common Prayer* of the Episcopal Church. "We bless thee (or thank thee) for our Creation." If Creation isn't an act of God, I don't know what is. We also thank God for our "preservation, for all the blessings of this life, but above all for thine inestimable love in the redemption of the world by our Lord Jesus Christ, for the means of grace, and for the hope of glory." I am convinced that these are acts of God. We call something a miracle, not because it can't be, but simply because we cannot understand it with our finite minds. If you are interested further in miracles, I would suggest C. S. Lewis' book titled, *Miracles*, which you can probably get at your local bookstore. That God created the universe out of nothing is, to my mind, a miracle; and having done that, I think we can expect God to perform a few more miracles, like the Incarnation. As Anglican theologian, Bishop Stephen Neal, has put it: "Liberal theology is only able to offer mankind a God who loved us a little, but not enough to become one of us, not enough to become man or human."

In further regard to the Incarnation—forgive me if I reminisce for a moment.

I used to wonder why God came into our world as He did? Why did the eternal word of God become flesh and dwell among us?

Strangely enough, the answer to that question came to me while I was a graduate student at the University of Madrid. The answer came to me—not at St. George's British Embassy Chapel where I began my ministry back in 1934, but in a bullring—at a "corrida de toros," or bull fight.

Bull fighting, you say, is a brutal sport. It is not unlike boxing where two men try to knock one another senseless. Sometimes one of them is killed or later suffers from irreversible brain damage.

I went out for boxing at Stanford University and soon discovered that there must be better ways of meeting young men of my age.

At this particular bull fight, the bull won! Fortunately, the matador or "torero" was not killed but tossed out of the ring into the stands.

The crowd roared their approval of the brave bull demanding that he be allowed to go free out to pasture. But the bull, still enraged and disoriented, refused. He didn't know he was free. Suddenly the gate at the other end of the ring opened and two oxen trotted in. They took their places on either side of the bull. The bull calmed down. He could relate to them. He trusted them, and in their company went out to freedom and to life

Suddenly I realized why God did what He did—why the eternal Creative Word became flesh, became Incarnate—or human—as one of us.

There is a tendency to complicate the Gospel. It is alleged that Jesus visited some theological students and asked them, "Who do people say that I am?" They replied, "Some say you are John the Baptist; others that you are Elija, still others say that you are a great teacher and even the prophet."

Jesus said, "But who do you say that I am?" They

replied, "You are the eschatological manifestation of the kerygma in which we find the prototypical standard for all our interpersonal relationships." And Jesus said, "Would you repeat that?"

What happened in that bullring and what the Gospel tells us in plain words is that the eternal word of God became Incarnate and that God truly was and still is in Christ reconciling the world to Himself.

I believe Jesus is the fullest manifestation of God's love. The Gospel proclaims that each human life is sacred. Everything we cherish; everything we can be proud of in our civilization we owe directly or indirectly to Jesus Christ. Even when we deny Him or ignore Him we live by His bounty. The industrial-strength atheist or perhaps some of the members of the A.C.L.U. owe more to Christ than they realize. Indeed, "the hinge of human history may be found on the door of that stable in Bethlehem."

We need to proclaim that Gospel today, to confess Christ as Lord and Savior, to show forth Christ in our lives and to see Him in all others.

Creation is an on-going process both physically and spiritually. It is God acting in and through His entire Creation. God is not finished with this world or any other part of His Creation. And that may shed some light on why we have volcanoes and earthquakes. God isn't finished with us either. We are God's unfinished business. He has business to do with us, and we are to cooperate with him in this. St. John the Evangelist refers to God's evolving spiritual purpose and the evolutionary development of His material creation in the prologue of his Gospel: "In the beginning was the Word, and the Word was God. All things were made by Him. In Him was life; and the life was the light of men." Then St. John speaks of God's witness, which culminates in Christ: "The word was made flesh. Christ was in the world, but not everyone received Him." This is true today. "But to them who received Him, who believe in his Name, gave He and gives He the power to become." In Hebrews 1:1-4, we also see the cosmic Christ, how He is revealed gradually through His Creation, the prophets, the religious seers of many religions, even through people like ourselves who lived before us, until we see Him, the Epiphany, the manifestation of God, "the Son of God, appointed heir of all things, through whom God created the world." This may shed light on what used to puzzle me: the words of Jesus, who said, "No one comes to the Father except by me."

People ask, "When will something higher than human life arrive on this planet?" I believe that something higher has already come and visited this planet in Jesus

Christ. The Gospel tells us that God was not simply like Jesus, but that He was and is in Christ, reconciling the world to Himself. Thus we see in the Scriptures that the disciples gradually came to realize that Jesus was more than a great teacher, a great prophet, a healer of mind, body, and soul. This has been my experience and maybe it has been yours too. At times I was a palagean. I didn't need grace. I could do it myself until I found out I couldn't. At times I was an Arian. But the more that I saw of Jesus and the closer that I came to Him, or He came to me, the more I came to believe in Him, as did St. Peter at Ceasarea Phillippi who said in answer to Jesus' question, "Who do you say that I am?" "Thou art the Christ, the Son of the living God."

To me it is reasonable to believe in an intelligent, loving Creator. It is reasonable to believe the best that we can about Him. And that best is revealed in Christ, where God's reconciling and redemptive love shines through most clearly. I agree with St. Anselm, theologian and Archbishop of Canterbury, who wrote in AD 1094: "God is that than which no higher can be conceived."

I accept Jesus as my Lord and Saviour and believe Him who said, "He who has seen me has seen the Father;" "Come unto me, all ye that travail and are heavy laden, and I will refresh you." "So God loved the world, that he gave his only begotten Son, to the end that all that believe in him should not perish but have everlasting life."

You may remember how the submarine, *Squallas*, made her last dive, and lay at the bottom of the Atlantic Ocean, 240 feet below. The crew sent up a buoy to mark the spot, and then waited and wondered and hoped and prayed. They knew they could not save themselves. Salvation would literally have to come from above. Let us not be worried by that word, salvation. We have hospitals and doctors and nurses to save us from disease. We have schools and colleges to save us from ignorance, etc. Believe me, there were no palageans aboard that submarine at that time. And salvation did come. Some 30 hours later, the crew of the *Sculpin* sent down a diving bell and rescued them a few at a time. It might be well to note that not one of the 33 men trapped in the stricken sub refused to be saved. Not one said, "I don't need to be saved. I can do it myself." Not one of them said, "There's too much to give up down here. I'll wait until I'm married and settle down." "I don't understand how this diving bell works." And then the excuse you have often heard, "There are too many hypocrites aboard the *Sculpin*." Nobody said that, not one of them. All gladly accepted the way of salvation, and all were saved. We can find salvation in Christ. Salvation really means release. Release from fear, release from anxiety, release from depression, release from loneliness, release from the bondage of destructive habits. The choice is ours. In Jesus' temptation in the wilderness, He refused to use force. He refused to use bribes to initiate or to extend His kingdom. The choice, therefore, is ours. There is no substitute for personal commitment, for betting our lives, our eternal future on Him who asks, "Who do you, John Jones or Jane Smith, say that I am?" Christianity is not simply a matter of knowing things about Jesus, but of receiving Him who seeks our commitment.

R. Heber Gooden

Christians have been falsely accused of worshipping three Gods, a "Committee God," so called, by those who object to the doctrine of the Holy Trinity. We often use the phrase: "In the Name of the Father, and of the Son, and of the Holy Spirit."

Why the doctrine of the Holy Trinity? This doctrine has been under fire since it was formulated at the council of Nicacea in A.D. 325 even by those who profess to be Christians. Thomas Jefferson wrote that, "When we shall have done away with the incomprehensible jargon of the Trinitarian arithmetic and got back to the pure and simple doctrine Jesus inculcated, we shall be truly and worthily his disciples." Obviously Jefferson misunderstood the meaning and purpose of this doctrine as do those today that claim that Christians worship three Gods, or a "Committee God", etc. Jefferson made the mistake of oversimplifying the nature and concept of God. Like others, he seemed to ignore what Jesus said of Himself and what His disciples came to believe about Him.

Among the "pure and simple doctrines that Jesus inculcated" was the uniqueness of His person and of God's revelation through Him. "He that hath seen me hath seen the Father." "So God loved the world, that He gave His only begotten son, so that all that believe in Him should have everlasting life." (St. John 3:16)

Clearly our Lord did not claim to be simply a great teacher or even the greatest person that ever lived.

When, after His Resurrection, He appeared to St. Thomas and invited him to touch the prints of the nails in His hands and the spear wound and Thomas declared, "My Lord and My God."

Jesus replied, "Because you have seen me you have believed. Blessed are those who have not seen me." Yes, we here today 2,000 years later, and have believed.

The Church does not and should not condemn those who honestly interpret Christian doctrine or cast the Christian faith in terms acceptable to their minds. But this does not mean that the Church should quietly and officially agree to any and all interpretations, like the politician who allegedly said, "There go my people, I must follow them for I am their leader."

Many have a Trinitarian experience of God without professing to have a Trinitarian mind. A thoughtful and earnest layman said to me, "I cannot accept the doctrine of the Holy Trinity. I believe God created the universe, I believe God is love because that is the best I can think of Him, and Jesus showed God's love. I can believe that God speaks to me in my conscience and helps me to do what is right." What he was saying is, "I believe in God as creator, as revealer, and as sanctifier." And it is this three-fold experience of God that the doctrine of the Holy Trinity does not attempt to explain but to take into account.

Any definition is influenced by the amount of knowledge and experience possessed by the person who attempts to define. When I was a little boy I liked frogs, even dried, pocket-sized frogs. My mother once told my father she felt like crossing herself before examining my pockets because she knew that the only thing that she would not find would be money. In that regard I guess she thought I was like my father: a clergyman with a large family seldom carries much cash in his pocket. At that time I may have liked frogs even more than girls, but as I grew up my values changed considerably. Obviously, any attempted definition of girls in my childhood would have been too simple and too unsympathetic.

When the universe seemed small and the earth was obviously flat and the sun smaller than the earth. and, of course, it revolved around the earth, a simple definition was adequate. When matter was considered a hard substance and the hydrogen atom was one of the smallest known to science and was inert and powerless, a simple definition was sufficient. The less we know about something the easier it is to define it in simple terms.

The person who will only accept or believe what he or she fully understands is in trouble. That person would not turn on the light because he or she would not know what energy is entirely. A man like that would never get married because, as Zsa Zsa Gabor, has put it, "There are three kinds of men who do not understand women; young men, middle-aged men, and old men."

There are three kinds of people who do not understand God fully: men, women, and children. But the Trinitarian is not guilty of over simplifying the nature of God in an effort to fit the infinite being into his finite mind. Conversely, the more we know about a person or a thing, the more complex or mysterious that thing becomes, and we accept these facts and have to include them in any definition simply because they are.

R. Heber Gooden

LOVE IS AN INTERPERSONAL RELATIONSHIP

We believe that God is love. Henry Kissinger said he didn't know as much as God, but he did know as much as God did at his age. He was joking. God is eternal—eternally wise and eternally loving. He didn't become wiser and more loving as He grew older, so to speak. For God's sake and for your own sake, let God be God. Love is not merely an ideal in isolation, a philosophical absolute. God was always love, He did not improve with age. Love is a relationship between persons. The Trinitarian concept of God as an interpersonal composite unity (that is, God in three persons) fits the belief in God as love eternal more than any other concept.

To illustrate further, there are two contradictory theories regarding the transmission of light: the wave theory and the photon theory. The fact of the radio proves the wave theory and the fact of television proves the photon theory. Images and sound: each seem logical to exclude the other. Nevertheless, both are right. This paradoxical situation is accepted by scientists and its acceptance is known as the "Principle of Complimentarity." Niels Bohr, who introduced the "Principle of Complimentarity" into physics gave as a theological example the complimentarity of God's mercy and justice.

Further, that God is both transcendent and immanent may seem paradoxical but it is verified by the facts of religious experience.

A God whom we could fully comprehend and explain—like a universe which the scientists could fully comprehend and explain—would be too small and too simple to be true.

The Doctrine of the Holy Trinity is Christianity's "Principle of Complimentarity." It tells us that "we don't have to wait until we get heaven into our heads before we try to get our heads into heaven." A quotation from G. R. Chesterton. A Bishop once examined a confirmation class before the Service. He happened to ask this question of a boy who had an impediment in his speech: "What is the Holy Trinity?"' The boy replied, "The Fah, the So, and Ho Go." The Bishop said, "I don't understand." The boy repeated it and the Bishop said, "I still don't understand." The boy then said as clearly as he could, "You aren't supposed to understand, it's a mystery."

The Doctrine of the Holy Trinity does not attempt to explain the infinite God but to preserve for us the three-fold Christian revelation and experience of God.

Christ did not make God understandable. He made Him lovable. Christ did not try to explain God's love. He showed it in the stable, on the Cross, through the empty tomb, and by the power of Pentecost.

Some people say that our Trinitarian belief about the fullness and richness of God's love is "too good to be true." I submit that it is too good not to be true.

Our life is a venture of faith. Why not take the highest faith we know? Why not accept with humble and grateful hearts the noblest revelation of God, believing that He is the fulfillment of prophecy and the answer to our deepest needs: creative mind, redemptive love, indwelling presence, Maker, Redeemer, Sanctifier of the people of God, Father, Son, and Holy Spirit, which is and ever shall be, one God, world without end.

Why Do Bad Things Happen To Good Chihuahuas?

You will recall my story about the untimely death of a Chihuahua puppy who fell asleep in an easy chair and was accidentally crushed by a young deacon. Even if that puppy had disobeyed an order not to get on the furniture he did not deserve capital punishment. He was a juvenile delinquent who had committed a misdemeanor.

However, the question we really ask is not a whimsical one. It is serious. The problem of evil and pain has caused some people to become atheists. That happened to me for a while. It has shaken the faith of many. Every philosophy and religion attempts to answer the question: "Why evil and suffering?"

I have taken courses in comparative religions and philosophy and make no claim to be an authority on these matters, although some of the books I have read on these subjects were written by recognized authorities. In my opinion, based on years of experience and a long pastoral ministry, the most compelling answer is found in the Christian faith. I refer to the cross on Calvary, which proclaims the reality and prevalence of sin and selfishness. It is also a sign of the amazing love of God which passes human understanding.

There is a ballad which was popular in the 1960s which I quote here:

> "Now Barabbas was a killer. And they let Barabbas go.
> But you are being crucified for nothing here below,

while God is up in heaven, but he doesn't do a
   thing.
With a million angels watching and they never
   move a wing."

This ballad is a protest against the apparent difference
between the character of God and the character of Jesus.
Jesus, the good man. Yes, even communists and atheists
call Jesus good. He is the best and noblest person that
ever lived on earth. He was crucified. And God, the
Father Almighty, Creator of all things visible and invisible, does nothing to intervene, to stop the tragedy.

We sympathize with those who wonder why an
Almighty God would allow evil and suffering in a
world he created.

Why does God allow these things to happen? Doesn't
he care?

Jesus said, "He that hath seen me hath seen the
Father." Christians believe that the cross on Calvary
says, "God was and is in Christ reconciling the world to
Himself." If you would understand the love of God it
would be through that cross. The cross makes us face
the facts about human sinfulness and God's love. It tells
us that we need help; that we are not self-sufficient, not
saints in need of promotion but sinners in need of
redemption.

One of my favorite authors is Mark Twain, although I
do not subscribe to some of his religious opinions. For
example, he once said that if he "ever joined a church it
would be the Episcopal Church because the Episcopal
Church was not concerned with either politics or religion!"

However, he certainly spoke the Gospel truth to the

man who sat next to him on the platform at a Fourth of July celebration in Hartford, Connecticut. That man had just fervently recited Henley's "Invictus," a poem that reeks of humanistic chauvinism. Twain leaned over to him and said, "So you are the master of your fate and the captain of your soul? Like hell you are!"

I've often been told by well-meaning people that the Church has made the simple religion of Jesus too complicated, and they say to me, "Just give me that good old 'Golden Rule'. That's all the religion I need!" Apparently, they need no help from God and no support group.

I'm tempted to reply: "All the astronomy I need is "twinkle, twinkle, little star" because without God's grace and love we could not even begin to keep the "Golden Rule." They imagine that they can enjoy the fruits of religion while ignoring and neglecting the roots.

What happened to the "Golden Rule" in Nazi Germany? Some people were not the right kind of people. Therefore the "Golden Rule" did not apply to them. What happened to the "Golden Rule" in Communist Russia? Millions were allowed to die of starvation on the newly collectivized farms. They were victims of a system that failed. Jesus said, "The Sabbath was made for man; not man for the Sabbath." The Soviet rulers believed otherwise. I used to wonder if the USSR didn't mean the Union of Silently Swallowed Republics. Thank heaven Herbert Hoover saved many of them by sending food from the United States.

Do we apply the "Golden Rule" to everybody in this country? Not yet.

The question is: "What is man?" "What is a human being?" Are we nothing more than a means to an end, a vote, a cog in some industrial machine, cannon fodder, a drop of blood in some dictator's ocean of racial purity, ants in a communal ant hill—or are we "children of God and inheritors of the Kingdom of Heaven?"

The answer to this question is basically religious. Arnold Toynbee, who is recognized as a leading modern historian, wrote: "Christianity is the midwife of Western Civilization because of its belief in the importance and intrinsic value of the human individual."

People may say, "I can understand or accept the suffering of the guilty; but why does God allow the innocent to suffer?"

Imagine the suffering of the parents of a son who killed himself while driving under the influence. Imagine them saying, "We couldn't care less. He had it coming to him!"

If God had made a world in which the innocent could never suffer, it would be a world without parents, brothers, sisters, children, husbands, wives, and friends. Would that be a better world than this?

God so loved the world that He chose to make a universe in which not all His creatures would be blindly subject to His laws like, rocks, trees, and the lower animals. If we refuse to love Him who first loved us, He suffers. That is why God's love must bear the sign of the cross.

Christianity did not invent sin or guilt, but no religion or philosophy takes a more objective look at sin and guilt than the religion which bears the sign of the cross. It is against the background of that cross that we can see our real need and begin to understand the amazing grace of God.

If this were a world full of sweetness and light, a romantic, crossless Christianity would suffice. If this were a world in which it would be natural to be good, a legalistic religion would be adequate. If this were a world in which materialism was the whole truth, then the possession of position and wealth would satisfy our needs.

The cross tells us that this is not that kind of world. Our greatest need is salvation. We need to be saved from self-centeredness and all that makes us reject God and neighbor.

A man once looked at a large crucifix in the church and asked, "If I'm all right and you're all right, what are you doing up there, Jesus?"

When Jesus looked down from the cross what did He see? Capitalists only? Communists only? Only Blacks, or whites, or browns, or any one particular race of people? Only Democrats, or Republicans, or only rich people, or poor people? He saw everyone. Sin is an equal opportunity employer.

Our world is not like a Western movie. I wish it were. People don't wear black hats or white hats. In this world it seems that everyone is running around dressed alike and often switching sides. Will Rogers was asked, "What is wrong with the world?" He replied, "I guess it's just people." The Bible says, "If we say we have no sin, the truth is not in us."

You could say that I'm your normal, run-of-the-mill homo sapien who is often tempted and frequently succumbs to it. Sometimes the easiest way to get rid of temptation seems to be to succumb to it. But we know that this does not end temptation. What we need is Grace. Now, when I tell the truth about myself some people who believe they know me very kindly say, "The dear Bishop is so modest." Actually, I'm just trying to be honest. We do the things that we ought not to do, and we do neglect to do the things that we ought to do. We need Grace. We need the support group, namely the Church or the body of Christ.

We know that the crowd clamored for the release of Barabbas and the crucifixion of Jesus, and they got their wish.

Recently I saw a bumper sticker that read, "God is not dead. He just doesn't want to get involved." Yet, nowhere does God seem to be more involved than on that cross. For us and for our salvation He came down—He suffered under Pontius Pilate—was crucified, dead, and buried. God is not, "up in heaven," simply watching and doing nothing. He is with us in our pain and He does not wait for us to deserve His love. He comes to us and offers us pardon and the means of Grace and the hope of glory.

Whenever love and goodness meet hate and evil, there has got to be a cross. Therefore, in the cross we see that there is no difference between the character of God and the character of Jesus. The love that we see in Jesus is God's love shining through. God was and is in Christ, reconciling the world to Himself. The cross tells us that God's love is down to earth. God is with us. He did not make our world easy or safe. We cannot demand complete sovereignty and then expect to be bailed out when things get difficult. We cannot have power to choose and automatically expect to be saved from the effects of our false choices. God made it possible for us to respond to His love, to grow spiritually, not only in this world but in life after death. Long before His death on Calvary, Christ said, "And I, if I be lifted up, I shall draw all people unto me." How, we do not know, but it has happened to millions and it happens today to those who will receive Him.

Time magazine published a moving article about an

airline stewardess named Mary Frances Housley. Over her picture was the caption: "She could have Jumped." When her plane skidded off the runway in Philadelphia and caught on fire, Frankie Housley quickly opened the door and stood inside helping the passengers to safety. She was ready to jump when a woman screamed, "Get my baby!" Frankie went back into the flaming interior of the cabin. There was an explosion. When the wreckage cooled the fireman found the body of Frankie Housely and four-month old Brenda Joyce Smith in her arms. She could have jumped. Our Lord said, "Greater love hath no one than this, that they lay down their life for a friend." He too, could have jumped. He could have avoided the cross, but He said, "Not my will but thine be done."

We know of those who have laid down their lives for their country, their loved ones, and for others. I have reason to believe that there are those whose father, mother, brother or sister, or other loved one did make that sacrifice who may be reading this. We thank God for such people, and for the safe return of those who were willing to take that risk. Jesus said, "Greater love hath no one than this, that they lay down their life for a friend. Ye are my friends."

Should this noblest form of love be possible to sinful humans and not to God? Is it beneath God's dignity to sacrifice Himself and to suffer for His creatures?

There are those who claim that God is above and beyond suffering and compassion. To them the cross is foolishness. If this be true, then Christ is wrong. If this be true then Jesus revealed a greater concept of God than that which God is. St. Anselm of Canterbury said or wrote, "God is that than which no greater can be conceived." It is not possible for us to think higher thoughts of God than what He is. Our souls do not vibrate to a note unsounded in the universe. Our Lord did not claim to be better than the Father. He said, "He who hath see me hath seen the Father."

Jesus shows us all we need to know about the Father and his love. It is our pride that made Good Friday necessary. It is God's love that refused to escape the cross. Pride is not something for us to stand on, but to step on. The cross reveals to us the true nature of sin, as senseless, thankless rebellion against God Himself—the attempt to abolish God. The cross also reveals to us the awful humility, the depth, the amazing compassion of the love of God. We do not see sin in its true light until we see it against the background of Calvary.

Thanks be to God that there also on Calvary we find God most clearly revealed as saving love, offering to all who will receive it with grateful and penitent hearts the power of His redemptive Grace.

R. Heber Gooden

WHERE DO CHIHUAHUAS AND OTHER PETS GO AFTER DEATH?

Many people ask that question. In the Anglican Communion and other communions and churches there are services for the "Blessing of the Animals." They are not christened, they are blessed. They are not members of any church but they are all God's creatures.

That Chihuahua was not a working dog. He couldn't guard junk yards, or sniff out drugs, or pull sleds, or bring slippers to his mistress, but he received and returned affection. He was faithful and devoted and grateful. It is said that older people with pet animals are apt to live longer and stay healthier mentally and physically. I can understand why people ask the question, "Where does my pet go after death?" I have officiated occasionally at the burial of pets on the request of their owners who are parishioners of mine. For me it is a pastoral opportunity. They have lost a companion. My prayer would be one of thanks to God for that blessing and for the grateful memories that the association with that creature have left behind.

There is nothing said in the scriptures about where pets go, but we believe that God who created all things visible and invisible will not neglect them. I like that hymn which is often sung in Sunday School:

All things bright and beautiful, all creatures great
and small;
All things wise and wonderful, the Lord God made
them all.
Each little flower that opens, each little bird that
sings

He made their glowing colors, He made their tiny
    wings.
He gave us eyes to see them and lips that we might
    tell
How great is God Almighty who has made all
    things well.

Many of us believe this, as indeed do I. It is a reasonable belief especially when we consider the alternative.

When You're Dead, You're Dead

A few years ago I boarded an Amtrak train at San Jose, California, to go to San Luis Obispo to see my children and grandchildren. It was a hot day in August. The generator stopped, the lights went off, the air conditioning ceased to work, the toilets didn't flush, the water didn't run. There was no way you could open the windows, and it got hotter, more humid and more suffocating as time went on. I groped my way in semi-darkness to the club car for a snack. An old man about my age was complaining bitterly in a loud voice and I heard him say that we were all going to die of suffocation. He then said, "But, when you're dead, you're dead." I said, "Are you?" "Of course," he replied. "What makes you so sure?" "Were you ever dead before?" And he replied, "Reverend, only a fool would imagine you could live after you die." "That's your opinion, not mine. That's your belief. Not everyone believes as you do." And then I went on to say, "You may be right, but you can't prove it. You'll just have to wait."

God intended for us to die. That's why death is so inevitable. But some of us may be like the American novelist, William Saroyan, who toward the end of his days on earth, said, "I always knew people died, but I thought that maybe in my case, God would make an exception."

He doesn't. But we don't have to die spiritually, and God doesn't want us to. It is more reasonable and logical to say, "I believe in the life everlasting" than in "death everlasting."

So much in the universe is alive. Even matter is

energy in motion. When Democritus, the materialist Greek philosopher, conceived the idea of the atom in 400 B.C. he did not know that there was anything smaller than the atom and did not know what science knows now, that the atom is not an indivisible, solid substance. It is more like a thought than a thing.

The Christian poet Robert Browning writes:

We find that great things
grow out of little things
and little things grow lessening
until at last God comes behind them.

This is a living universe. Jesus said, "God is the God of the living, not of the dead." The miracle is not that we should live after death, but that we should be alive now; not that we should be given spiritual bodies for life beyond death, but that now we should be Temples of the living soul for this present existence.

The structure of the bird within the egg would be meaningless unless there would come the chance to fly and sing. What is the point of producing powers which can never be used?

We have a spiritual nature and spiritual aspirations which can not be fulfilled in a purely materialistic universe or within this life only.

The very rationality of the universe requires eternity and spiritual purpose. Our ultimate destiny is not dust but life eternal.

For every universal longing there is a reality to satisfy it. For hunger—food. Hunger did not invent food. We rightly blame ourselves for wasting the resources of our planet and polluting our environment. If death ends all, if the most valuable thing we know of, human personality, is annihilated at death, God is the most wasteful of all. I cannot believe that He could be guilty of such poor ecology.

Our Christian faith tells us that the best in the universe is a revelation of the deepest in it; and it will not be thrown away.

Le compte du Nouy, in his book, *The Soul of the Universe*, writes, "The soul does not vibrate to a note unsounded in the universe."

To me the greatest miracle is Jesus Christ. His birth, His life, His death, His rising again, the coming of the Holy Spirit.

St. Paul may not refer to the empty tomb; yet he believed in the risen Lord because he met Him and his life was transformed by that encounter. So he said, "If Christ be not risen from the dead we are of all people, most miserable."

The desperate disciples who saw Christ die on the cross were made radiant and courageous by the presence of the risen Lord. Something happened to them on that first Easter Day, and they were never the same afterwards. Something still happens. The Church throughout the world bears witness to this and we celebrate it every first day of the week which is a celebration of the Resurrection.

In Jesus' life, death, Resurrection and in the presence of the Holy Spirit, we have the revelation of the amazing love of God.

In the discovery of the love of God is our assurance of the life everlasting. We have reason to believe that in the love of Christ the universal pattern shows through.

The Scottish poet and mystic, George McDonald, wrote an epitaph:

Here lie I, Martin Elginbrod;
have mercy on my soul, Lord God,
As I would do were I Lord God
And thou were Martin Elginbrod.

Jesus said, "If ye, being evil or imperfect, know how to give good things to your children, how much more shall not your heavenly Father?" He also said, "He who hath seen me hath seen the Father."

Our fellowship with him can never end, and nothing can separate us from the love of God which He has manifested in Christ Jesus, our Lord. Be sure that God, who has given us this life will enable us to reach in safety the next stage in our pilgrimage.

I am not suggesting a superficial optimism. In my ministry to people in crises such as terminal illness and death, I have been aware of unseen resources upon which some people are able to draw in time of stress and need. I have often been ministered to more than I have ministered.

My favorite drive in Shreveport, Louisiana, is Fairfield Avenue in the depth of winter. Those beautiful old oaks, their leafless limbs etched against the leaden sky, look dead—but actually they are very busy living—quietly communing with God's earth, sky, air, and sun.

The late Presiding Bishop, Arthur Lichtenberger, sent out an Easter message from which I quote: "During His life and death and Resurrection, Christ has opened to us the gate of everlasting life which means that He has opened up new possibilities of life now. But a gate leads nowhere for us unless we walk through it. The fact of Christ means nothing in our lives unless we respond to it, my Lord and my God!"

I once read a poem which reminds me of how some people think we should live:

> *There once was a cautious girl*
> *Who never romped or played.*
> *She never drank, she never smoked,*
> *from the path she never strayed.*
> *So when she passed away*
> *the insurance was denied*
> *for since she never really lived,*
> *they claimed she never died."*

I am not advocating a life of hedonism. Some of us know that if you live it up you have to live it down. Jesus was in favor of living. He said, "I have come that you may have life more abundantly—a life of spiritual growth and of service to God and neighbor."

A little child once prayed:

> *"Now I lay me down to sleep.*
> *I pray the Lord my soul to keep.*
> *If I should wake before I die."*

That child made no mistake. Precisely, we ought to wake up before we die. Here and now we can keep our lives open on the Godward side, becoming increasingly aware of His presence and grateful to Him for our creation, preservation, and all the blessing of this life. Above all, for His inestimable love in the redemption of the world through our Lord Jesus Christ, for the means of Grace and for the hope of glory.

As Soon As We're Born, We're Old Enough To Die

That is probably the last thing that we'll do on earth. Benjamin Franklin said that nothing is more certain than death and taxes. However, death has not gotten any worse. To be or not to be is still the question, and it is very important how we face this question; for the way we face death influences the way we face life here and now.

Our Lord never gave us a guarantee as to how long we would live here. He did promise abundant life here and everlasting life on the other side of death.

You may have heard this epitaph on the tombstone of an infant:

Since I was so quickly done for
I wonder what I was begun for!

Some people try to escape that question. They refuse to talk or think about death, and when a loved father dies they dress him in a tuxedo and place him in a metal box as though he were asleep, when we all know that most men do not go to sleep in a tuxedo in a metal box.

The validity of every philosophy, ideology, and religion, depends on how it answers the question, "Is death the end?" There is a tomb in Red Square where the chief saint of communist Russia lies embalmed all dressed up and made up and no where to go, at least officially. That is the closest to life everlasting you can get in Soviet Russia. But as Tanya and Ivan, little brothers of the so called people's republic, stand shivering in line—to view Lenin's remains and get credit for this gesture of patriotism, do they not also ask themselves the age-old question, "If a man dies, shall he live again?"

No "bread alone" philosophy or "this world only" philosophy will ever satisfy our innate longing for ultimate meaning, worth, and purpose. My father lived to be almost 102 years of age and on his 100th anniversary he was looking over the funeral arrangements that he had made: all Easter hymns. He wished his funeral to be joyful. His only disappointment was the rapid turnover of his proposed pallbearers. He discovered that he had already buried most of them and when I said, "Father, why didn't you appoint young men?" He said, "I did. They were all in their early 70s." My father, together with others including myself, celebrate another tomb, the empty tomb at Jerusalem, where Christ demonstrated that death could no more have dominion over Him, over us, if we accept the living, risen Lord.

Apostolic Christianity understood its faith in the light of the good news of Easter. Dying on the cross on Good Friday was not the last thing Jesus did. And that is why we have the Christian Church today.

It is an historical fact that Jesus lived, was tried under Pontius Pilate, was crucified, died, and was laid in a tomb, and that tomb was sealed and a special guard mounted by the authorities.

The story of the early morning visit to the empty tomb has the ring of truth about it. The women went there to embalm a corpse. They were skeptical and they were frightened when they saw someone at the entrance of the tomb whom they assumed to be the gardener. A good assumption. Who else would be in the garden at that early hour? Besides, nobody, not even then, rose from the dead! It was no easier to believe that a dead person could rise from the dead in AD 30 than it is today.

What changed their minds? They became certain that He was alive. They talked with Him, and they ate with Him. And St. Paul (writing at a time when the resurrection news was as contemporary, as let us say, the assassination of John F. Kennedy), said that the risen Lord was seen by many people in many places and even by 500 people at once, many of whom were still alive at the time. (I Corinthians 15:6)

They were so convinced that they were willing to preach the Resurrection at the risk of persecution, torture, and even death. Many, including Peter and Paul, suffered martyrdom.

The Jewish and Roman authorities were embarrassed by the rumor that Christ had risen. They looked in vain for the body. I read a latter day graffiti which said, "Easter has been canceled. The body has been found."

A book was published about 15 years ago in England entitled, *The Passover Plot*. It was a rehashing of some of the arguments offered to refute or discredit the Christian claim regarding the Resurrection. These arguments have come to us through the centuries since that first Easter morning. The author of this book is Hugh J. Schonfield. Another book was published in London for the Book Club. It thoroughly and logically refutes these and all arguments that tried to discredit or cast doubt on the reality of the Easter event. It was written by Frank Morrison, entitled *Who Moved The Stone?* I do not know whether it is still available but I have it in my library.

The disciples would have never given their lives for a

lie. The Resurrection is as reliable a fact of ancient history as any other accepted fact.

You can say, "The Resurrection is a miracle, and I don't believe in miracles." That's your hang-up—your unproved prejudice. What you are saying is that you refuse to believe that anything can happen that has never happened before. How about this universe? There was a time when it was not. The age of matter can be computed by radiation. If the universe had always existed, the radiation would have died out long ago. Furthermore, the fact that science can compute the age of rocks does not do away with the "Rock of Ages." How about you and me? Each one of us is a unique creature; even identical twins are not exactly the same. There has never been nor will there ever be a person just like you. You are something special, and so is your neighbor. In that sense we are miracles—special children of God who made us.

On Good Friday Christianity faced the darkest and hardest questions. Easter is God's answer to these questions.

Almighty God, who created all things, was able to conquer hatred, sin, and death. Therefore we can face life with hope and believe it is worthwhile, and know that because God raised Jesus from the dead, the best is not at the mercy of the worst.

Some scientists have said that the odds against the "accident theory" are one to a number which, if written out in full would encircle the earth thirty-five times at the equator. Atheism is a bad bet. They say that horse sense is what keeps horses from betting on the human race. Imagine, if you can, 30,000 horses watching about

20 human beings run around the race track! Common sense ought to keep us from betting our lives on the illogical belief that everything just happens.

R. Heber Gooden

WHY WASN'T I ON THAT PLANE?

Some of us are not so quickly done for, and we may wonder why we're still here. Many years ago, I believe it was in 1950, I was waiting for my flight on Avianca Airlines in Medellín, Colombia, to visit our mission in Bogotá. My host, Arthur Taylor, who had an air cargo company called "El Burrito," was with me at the airport. The flight was announced but I was told that there was no space for me. Apparently, someone who was considered more important than I took my space. Of course, I was annoyed and protested. This was no pleasure trip. I had made that reservation two months ago to visit our 13 missions in that country. "Padre, lo sentimos mucho pero así es." "Father, we're very sorry, but that's the way it is." That evening as I was preparing for dinner at Arthur Taylor's home, my host knocked at my door, saying, "Bishop, you don't know how lucky you are. This report just came over my aviation radio. That plane crashed in Manizales, and they say—no survivors." I sent a cable to my wife telling her that I was alive and well and continuing with my schedule the next day.

Why wasn't I on that plane? I'm still not sure; but I know that God did not love me more than He did the others. He died and rose again for all of us—not just for Bishops!

More recently I visited a young man who was dying of AIDS at LSU Medical Center. His father said to me, "Why couldn't I die instead? I'm much older and I've lived my life." "Frankly, sir, I don't know. I don't know how I got to be 80 years old yesterday."

"Maybe the man upstairs doesn't need you," he

replied. "He needs me right where I am. He needs all of us right where we are, including you."

God is the God of life and growth. Our human life began in our mother's womb. There we were prepared for life after birth. Here in the womb of this world—in life on this planet—we are—or should be, with God's grace—developing spiritually for that greater life beyond the grave.

The approach of death is not the beginning of the end but only the end of the beginning of a life that goes from strength to strength in joyful service in God's kingdom.

St. Paul said, "If ye then be risen with Christ, think on those things that are above. Whatsoever things are good and noble and loving, concentrate on these." Live in the risen Christ now. Let not your hearts be troubled. Don't worry about what the future holds, think about Him who holds the future and whose redemptive love has been fully revealed in Jesus Christ and know that nothing—not even death—can ever separate us from that love.

I was asked this recently by a woman who was giving me a pedicure. It seems that as I grow older my feet get further away! From time to time I need a little help for them.

She had told me of the various jobs she had held. Hers was an interesting and helpful life to date. She asked me the question, "What do you do besides preach?" Actually, I try not to preach more than 20 minutes, although I often preach two or three times on a Sunday. Most congregations prefer short sermons, and this goes for commencement addresses and others.

There is the story of the Bishop who didn't know when or where to stop in his sermons. This was embarrassing to the rector or priest in charge of the parish or mission that the Bishop was visiting officially. It would have been fine to have a bumper congregation present for the Bishop, but his reputation for long sermons kept people away.

One day there was just a handful of the faithful present in the large nave of the church. The Bishop asked the rector after the service, "Didn't you tell the people I was coming?" He replied, "No, but it must have leaked out!"

Yes, I have preached thousands of times, mostly in Spanish in Latin America. I'll not forget the time I had the privilege of preaching on the Royal yacht with her Britannic Majesty Queen Elizabeth II and Prince Philip in the front row of the ship's lounge as the ship was in Miraflores locks near the end of her transit of the Panama Canal.

I was given this privilege because I was the Anglican Bishop of the Diocese that they were in at the time. It was suggested that I not speak for more than 10 minutes because her Majesty was on a tight schedule. To me, a royal suggestion is a command. In nine minutes the sermon was over. Chaplain Waters of the Royal Navy read the service and Admiral Sir Able Smith read the lesson. The Queen sang the hymns beautifully.

I have traveled over 500,000 miles in everything from a jumbo jet to a dugout canoe with my crosier or pastoral staff, which I call my typical, tropical, portable, collapsible, Episcopal, pastoral staff. Of all the means of transportation, the one I least prefer is the horse. Why should an animal so full of hay be so hard at the same time! I have slept in palaces—real ones, even ones with drawbridges—by invitation of the owners. Also in inns and "Posadas," and the homes of clergy and assorted hotels and in mud huts with palm thatched roofs and even in a jungle hammock! All this and other things in addition to preaching sermons. Speaking further of dugout canoes, or "cayucos," we had one that was about 25 feet long with a five-foot beam partly covered and powered by a Lister marine engine—maximum speed, seven knots. This was our means of transportation from Bluefields, Nicaragua, to Miskito Indian Missions along the Atlantic coast. To reach the village of Tabapauni, 50 miles away, we had to go through creeks and two lagoons including Pearl Lagoon. It took about 12 hours.

Archdeacon Waldock and I were ready to return to Bluefields after a 10-day visit to the missions when a young Indian woman whom I had confirmed the evening before asked me if we could take her and her husband to Bluefields to be with her parents and to see a doctor. She was very pregnant. I was reluctant to let them aboard but she assured me that the baby would not arrive for at least two weeks—so she said! You guessed it, we reached the point of no return when she started to have contractions. As in the case of the deacon and the dowager's Chihuahua, the seminary never prepared us for these things. I found myself asking as you may well have asked yourselves, "God why did you let this happen in the middle of nowhere? I never asked to be a Bishop and I do not need this." I believe He must have heard us because nobody panicked. We brewed some tea, my English Archdeacon's favorite beverage. Between contractions the expectant mother drank some. We all did, and we prayed together.

Fortunately, the baby did not arrive before we reached Bluefields Harbor. We put the mother in a cart and pushed her up the hill to the doctor's house where he took her into his office. As we were enjoying a cold beer in his parlor, we heard a baby cry. It was a boy.

What has this to do with religion or theology? A lot. That baby's cry was another of God's miracles. God kept us calm during our journey and we were glad to be safely home in Bluefields, Nicaragua.

R. Heber Gooden

There are many Advents. You have heard of the
Second Coming, that time when Christ will come in
power and glory to judge the world both the living and
the dead. The "Church's Teaching Series" includes a
book entitled *The Faith of The Church* by Pike and
Pittenger. On page 165 we read, "When will be the
Judgment? At the end of time." But, while time shall
come to an end, eternity does not just then begin. We are
at present in life eternal.

It is true that what we go after here determines where
we will go hereafter. Therefore, there are many Advents.

The first Advent was the coming of Christ in great
humility at Christmas.

Phillips Brooks described it so beautifully in his
hymn, "O Little Town of Bethlehem:"

How silently, how silently,
The wondrous gift is given!
So God imparts to human hearts
The blessings of His heaven.
No ear may hear His coming
But in this world of sin
Where meek souls will receive Him,
Still the dear Christ enters in.

Thank God that His first Advent to us in the Incarnate
Word has given us a choice. He did not overwhelm us
as He will in the final Advent or at the last coming. In
the last coming we will have absolute, ultimate, undeni-
able proof of His existence and His nature.

We would not be able to love God in that case because no one can be obliged or forced to love anyone—

not even to love God. Love has to be a free and willing response. So it is today.

I believe that it may be God's will that we cannot in this world prove the truth or falsity of Christianity or any of its alternatives.

In this world it isn't just the religious person who must live by faith. It's everybody, including the scientists.

Albert Einstein said, "Science is based on a postulate—a belief that the universe is law-abiding and amenable to thought."

I've heard the argument that there are so many different concepts about the nature of God, that probably there is no God at all. Some people believed the earth was flat and some still do. Others believe the earth is round, but flat like a pancake. Others, that it is round like a ball. Does that prove that there is no earth at all? The scientist cannot prove scientifically that his wife and children love him. He has to accept that on faith.

St. Anselm of Canterbury wrote, "God is that than which no higher can be conceived." We cannot think higher thoughts of God than what He really is: a reasonable belief, but it is still based on faith.

Thomas Henry Huxley, who lived in the latter half of the last century in England, was a biologist, a writer, and an outstanding exponent of Darwinism. Also he was an agnostic. It is said that one Sunday morning when he was a visitor in the home of some devout Church of England friends, the family invited him to come to church with them. He politely declined, but asked their oldest son if he would stay and tell him about his Christian faith. The son replied, "You could knock down all my arguments in a few seconds." Huxley answered, "I don't wish to argue with you. I really want you to tell me what Jesus means to you."

The young man did. And with tears in his eyes, Thomas Huxley said, "I'd give my right hand to have your faith."

It's easier to argue about God than to receive Him. We do not prove the reality of God merely by argument. That young man had met and experienced God in Christ. As Phillips Brooks put it, "When meek souls will receive Him, still the dear Christ enters in."

Jesus comes to us today, He speaks to us in the voice of our conscience, in prayer and worship, in the Bible; yes—believe it or not—and in the sermon, and, I hope, in this book.

He meets us in church and at the communion rail, as He promised. He still comes to us in humility and as our friend and companion. Here in lowly form He comes to us as He did in the manger, as He stood before Pilate, as He went up on the cross. He is still content to be among us in this world to give us time to choose for or against Him and time to repent; time to learn to love Him even as He first loved us.

Advent is a time, therefore, for preparation. Now is the acceptable time.

You recall Jesus' parable of the "Great Supper" in St. Luke, Chapter 14, "Come, for all things are ready. And they all with one accord began to make excuses." What flimsy, what ridiculous excuses!

Remember that our Lord is telling this story to a group of farmers or plantation owners. One farmer said, "I can't come because I have bought a piece of land and

I must see it." Can you imagine buying land without seeing it first, and passing up a free meal to view it in the dark!

Are you ready for this? Another farmer said, "I have bought five yoke of oxen and I go to prove them." Five yoke of oxen. That's 10 oxen! That was a major investment—like buying a used combine or harvester without seeing it first and now he says, "I can't come to your free dinner, with drinks on the house, because I've got to test drive my equipment in the dark."

Jesus had a marvelous sense of humor. His listeners must have been howling with laughter—but Jesus was making a serious point, these people were invited to enter the kingdom and they could not accept because they had other interests on this earth.

Now is the acceptable time. It may not always be a convenient time, but we must choose now before it is too late.

Former Presiding Bishop Sherrill told the story about the irascible old man who on his death bed asked to be baptized. The priest said, "Do you promise to renounce the devil and all his works?" "Now listen, Father, this is no time or place for me to be making enemies with anybody anywhere!"

I don't suppose there is ever a convenient time to have a baby. The most wonderful baby in the world was born at a most inconvenient time; his parents were on a journey by donkey to pay income tax. Children were not deductible. Jesus was born in a stable or a cave, and placed in a manger in the little town of Bethlehem.

Thank God He did not wait for a convenient time to come to us at that first Advent. We can be grateful that

He did not wait until we were ready to receive Him or good enough to deserve His love. There was no reservation made for them at the royal suite at the Bethlehem Hilton—no mayor, no city council, no municipal band to greet Him and Mary and Joseph.

As Bishop Brooks said, "When meek souls will receive Him, still the dear Christ enters in."

He still comes to us in malnourished children with bloated bellies, in street people, in abused children and women and even men, in oppressed, needy, and forsaken people. Also He comes in those who are relatively or seemingly all right but who need understanding, compassion, companionship. They may even be members of our church or our own family.

In the parable of the sheep and the goats, the judge says, "I have met you all before." "Oh, no, your honor, we never saw you before." "Yes, you did. I was a stranger and you gave me the cold shoulder. I needed clothing and you didn't give me anything to protect me from the cold. I was sick and in prison and you didn't visit me. I wanted to talk to you and you wouldn't bother to listen to me. Since you didn't do that to them, you didn't do it to me."

You will note that in this parable, the judge doesn't decide which are the sheep and which are the goats. He merely separates them. They were already sheep or goats. They had chosen to be sheep or goats when they had a chance to make that decision here on earth on their own. Indeed, where you go hereafter depends on what you go after here.

Here on earth there are many Advents. They are decisive. *The Book of Common Prayer* says that, "We are to seek Christ in all people." So—we meet Jesus every day in many ways. Now is time to see Him and to receive Him.

Plato, the philosopher who lived some 24 centuries ago, said there are three kinds of atheists. The professing atheist, like Madeline Murray O'Hare is no threat to the Church in this country, where some 98 percent of the people claim to believe in God. All of us can think of more reasons for believing than for not believing in God. For us, the former conflict between religion and science is no longer relevant. Why not count your blessings with a calculator? So, I am not going to waste your time by scratching you where you don't itch.

Let's talk about the other types of atheists who are more harmful and insidious because they claim to believe in God, and they may honestly think they do.

I will preface the description of these two type of God-fearing atheists by saying, "The stories you are about to hear are true, the names have been changed to protect the guilty."

Take, for example, Mr. and Mrs. Spiffledorfer. If you, dear reader, bear the name of Spiffledorfer, it has to be sheerly coincidental! The Spiffledorfers go to church with some regularity and also contribute to some extent. The God who was once active in Bible days, now dozes between the pages of Holy Scripture. God, for the Spiffledorfers is remote and irrelevant. He does not live in them. They are practical atheists. They have no God for today.

The worst atheists are, let us say, Mr. and Mrs. Smythe. The Smythes have made God in their own image; same race, economic and social class, nationality, political party, and religious denomination. God has no right to expect or demand much of them. They do not have to seek and serve Him in everyone but only in a select few. Maybe He owes them more than they owe Him.

They have given to God, country, and university; expect all three to be duly grateful. God should pay good dividends on their investment. For their support of Church and charity they own a "piece of the rock." In this case, the "Rock of Ages!"

Nobody owns God. Nobody really owns anything. If you think so, how much will you own 50 or more years from now? Or, are you planning to be the richest person in the cemetery?

To believe in God is to be a committed person. It is tempting to try to be a part-time Christians in a full-time world. Full commitment is a matter of priorities. The problem is not so much a lack of money, or time, or talent, but a sort of spiritual energy crisis. There simply cannot be a shortage of Grace. All of us are spiritual millionaires if we affirm God's Grace in our lives as heirs of God and joint heirs with Christ. But we are not always aware of the true nature and purpose of our lives.

In the early days of my Episcopate, I received a radiogram from the manager of the United Fruit Company in Colombia, South America, telling us of the sudden death of my archdeacon in Santa Marta. I went there to bring his body back to the Canal Zone for cremation in accordance with the wishes of his widow.

You won't believe the problems involved in taking a body out of Colombia! When the red tape seemed to weigh about as much as the crate, we were ready to go by barge through the Ciénaga to Barranquilla and thence by ship to Cristóbal via Puerto Limón, Costa Rica.

Because the captain of the barge feared the superstitions of his passengers, they painted my name on the crate but forgot to paint out the crosses indicating that it contained a body. Fortunately, the passengers assumed that the crate contained a statue of the Blessed Virgin Mary, and this made them very happy. It made me happy too. The big problem was, when the government agent at the port asked me, "Cuánto es el valor de la mercancía?" "What is the value of the merchandise?" Tell me, now, what is a dead body worth? "Ninguno." "No value."

We brought nothing into this world; it is certain we can carry nothing out. " The Lord gave and the Lord has taken away. Blessed be the name of the Lord." That's the way it was then, and that's the way it is now.

As Christians we have nothing to fear, so we can say, "Thanks be to God who has given us the victory through Jesus Christ."

On his 100th birthday, my father was honored by a reception hosted by the women of the Diocese of Los Angeles. Over a thousand people came to congratulate this retired Suffragan Bishop of Los Angeles who had touched their lives during his long and active ministry.

As I was driving him home, I said, "Father, that was a great outpouring of affection. I don't think you'll be able to top this." He replied, "Heber, before I go to bed tonight, I'm going to say a prayer: Oh, God, please make me humble, because as you doubtless know, I am a very important man." He was being his usual modest, whimsical self, but he spoke the truth. He was indeed a very important person. In fact all of us are very important to God, and that is really what matters. We are children of God by adoption and Grace. This is what gives us meaning and hope and purpose now. Death was universal long before the H-bomb. We cannot in this life only reach the end for which we were made. "Flesh and blood cannot inherit the kingdom of God." We must undergo change by being open to the spirit, renewed by the spirit.

The fundamental error is to forget who and why we are. The basic sin is to worship anything, even the best things—anything other than God. The change must begin here in this life. Here and now we must be increasingly dying to self, losing our lives in order to find them.

We have so much for which to be thankful. We are in God's debt for all the blessings of this life, "For his inestimable love in the redemption of the world by our Lord Jesus Christ, for the means of Grace and for the hope of glory."

Toward the beginning of this book, I stated that belief is not optional. It is not a luxury. It is essential. Everyone is a believer, although we don't all believe alike.

Life is not a question of to believe or not to believe. Inasmuch as we have to believe, why not believe the best we can? Let no one be ashamed to believe the best that he or she can believe; to accept the faith that gives the fullest and most meaningful answer to his or her life. Let us not be ashamed to say, "Lord, I believe, help thou my unbelief." You and I cannot help but believe. Living is believing, and the richest and fullest lives are those based on the deepest and fullest faith. However, belief is more than intellectual assent. I suspect that my readers who are married did not get married for purely intellectual reasons. I can tell you that I didn't know what science, or religion, or art, or marriage is until we have committed ourselves to these. So much of life is like a stained-glass window. How can you really ever appreciate a stained glass window until you come inside? To wait until we believe that we know all about our belief is just to let life pass us by, as I said, living is believing and believing is living. The best life is the commitment of ourselves, mind, body and soul, to the very highest belief that we know.

Let us beware of the little Gods that make people's lives shallow and make us small. Let us beware of the little minds that are capable of worshipping or believing only that which they can fully understand. Beware the substitutes for God in the faith of our fathers. These can never take the place of Him who is the Creator of all things visible and invisible, and who has taught us to take ourselves and all other persons seriously, not as a mere means to an end, not as compost or some earthly garden of Eden that will never bear fruit, but as people whom God takes seriously. Seriously enough to create us; seriously enough to reveal Himself to us in Christ; and to give us a living soul; to give us a freedom which enables us to love Him and our neighbor as ourselves. It is He whose love for us will not stop when our hearts stop beating in this world. May God grant us this faith. May He strengthen us in our commitments to it, because, in this faith our lives are going to have their greatest significance and worth now and forever.